ಹಿ

Table of Contents

   It signifies to us the mystery of the union between Christ and his Church and Holy Scripture commends it to be honored among all people.

   Dearly beloved: We have come together in the presence of God to witness and bless....

   ...that each may be to the other a strength in need, a counselor in perplexity, a comfort in sorrow, and a companion in joy.

   Give them wisdom and devotion in the ordering of their common life.

   Give them grace, when they hurt each other, to recognize and acknowledge their fault, and to seek each other's forgiveness and yours.

   ...with all that I am, and all that I have, I honor you.

Preface

Welcome to *The Marriage Journey*. This book is by ordinary Christians, for ordinary Christians in ordinary congregations. We are not professional marriage counselors, scholars, or experts in the field. We are a married couple, committed to our marriage and to our faith. We have written this book out of our own experience and will share with you what we have learned, sometimes in the school of hard knocks!

Some of our experience has come from our own marriages (his, hers, and ours); some of it comes from our experience with the marriages of others. Linda is an Episcopal priest and has counseled couples preparing for marriage and those already married. She is currently the Executive Director of LeaderResources, an Episcopal consulting and publishing organization, and has worked with congregations and dioceses to develop education and training programs.

Del is a Vice-President of the DuPont Company and has worked with people as they have faced various family-related issues, especially as those issues relate to their work life. While Linda is the writer on the team, Del is the person who most clearly articulates the spiritual dimensions of the issues. As an African American and the father of two young adult sons, he is also the one most in touch with realities of life in corporate America outside the professional life of the church.

Both of us have been confidants and supporters of countless friends, co-workers, and family members as they contemplated marriage or sought to build their marriage. Both have been through the pain of divorce and spent considerable time hesitating over whether we wanted to risk marriage again! In addition, we are an interracial couple who have lived in the United States and Canada and have experienced the challenges of being "different" in those cultures. These are the life experiences we bring to this book. You will hear and see some of our story; we invite you to share your story with each other and with other Christians who can support you on the way.

Our marriage has been like a journey in many ways, with new adventures unfolding daily. That journey began before we decided to formalize our relationship. Our marriage, in fact, began before we even realized it was underway! But once we became aware of the importance of this relationship in our lives and made a conscious decision to commit ourselves to this mutual journey, the trip took on new dimensions.

Since few of us would begin a journey without some preparation and adequate consideration for the training, provisions, and assistance required, as we began our marriage journey we assembled what we needed immediately and identified what we would need in the days and years ahead. That process of assembling information and support and of identifying issues and needs is an important part of making the marriage journey successful.

Finally, marriage is a communal, not a solitary, journey. Our partner is our primary traveling companion, but many others will be on the road with us, including clergy, family members, friends, and members of the Christian community. And remember…it is a *journey*. We haven't arrived and we don't expect that you will have arrived yet either. Being on a journey implies that you know where you want to go and that you're making progress in getting there; this book will give you a chance to develop your ideas of what direction you want to go and of how you're going to get there. We invite you to join us and other fellow travelers in the marriage journey as we all live and grow in love, learning from one another along the way.

How to Use This Book

There are many ways for different people to use this book for different purposes. Here we outline some of those ways, and we encourage you to experiment with your own. Each chapter is intended both for couples preparing for marriage and for those who have been married a few months or years. Within each set of chapter questions you will find one group of questions directed to the couple (divided into two sections for marriage preparation and marriage enrichment) and one for use in a group. You may find that you want to consider your responses to the questions separately before discussing them as a couple or in the group.

The projects and questions are designed to be extensive; they will not fit everyone. For example, in one project we encourage you to build a family tree and look at patterns that emerge. Del, as an African American, was unable to do that, as much of his family history is lost to him; working on his family tree is a painful reminder of that. Discussing how he felt about it was more important for us to do than completing the project.

As you read each chapter, pick those projects and questions that fit your situation or that call your attention to something you haven't thought about before. Adapt them, if you face special circumstances. If it doesn't apply to you or it is something you've already discussed *ad nauseam*, skip it! The purpose of the time you spend exploring these topics is for you to learn more about yourself, each other, and the marriage process so you can make informed decisions as you move more deeply into your relationship with each other.

If you and your partner are of the same sex, many, if not most, of the questions and issues raised in these chapters will apply to you. Different faiths and denominations have different approaches to the validity of such relationships: we do not address these issues here, as they are beyond the scope of this book. We simply assume that same-sex couples choosing to use this book will adapt the questions and discussions as appropriate.

⁋ For Couples Planning to Marry

You can use this book by yourselves, reading and discussing each chapter in course. This works best when both of you are enthusiastic about working together in this way and are fairly disciplined. Many people find it helpful to have some set schedule and at least one other couple doing it with them; otherwise, the busyness of getting ready for the wedding may derail you. A couple or an individual trying to decide if they in fact want to get married will also find this book helpful.

⁋ For Couples Already Married

You can use this book with just the two of you reading and discussing it at home. For example, it would be an appropriate way to prepare for a wedding anniversary. Plan to finish a few days before the anniversary and really celebrate who you are and what you have.

You might also want to read it if your marriage preparation was very brief and inadequate. You might find it most helpful if you've been married for at least eighteen months. By that point the honeymoon is over and reality has set in. Even if your marriage preparation was thorough, and even if you lived together for some time before the wedding, this is the time you will find many of these topics relevant.

⁋ For Congregations

Couples may want to gather as a group to work through this book. A group of friends or a mix of couples of differing years of experience with marriage would be appropriate. Decide beforehand whether the group will be study-oriented (one hour, discuss topic only) or support-oriented (two hours, discuss your experiences). This will determine who you ask to lead the group, how you structure the group, and what questions you use.

If an ordained or professional person is part of the group, don't feel that this person necessarily has to lead the group. The couple married longest might lead it or someone who is accustomed to leading groups. Or, you can rotate the leadership and just follow the questions as they are printed in the book.

If you regularly meet with a book study group, you might consider using this book, though it is important to adjust the questions to fit the less intimate setting. Focusing on the topic will make the questions less personal.

You may want to organize a married couples' retreat using some chapters or parts of the book (depending on how much prior reading couples do and how much time you have). In this case it would be helpful to have group leaders with some leadership skills and experience. You may wish to confer with your clergy in planning such a retreat.

If you plan to use the book as part of a study group, support group, or retreat, read the section "Organizing and Leading Groups" in the appendix. In the list of resources we have also identified training programs and married couple retreat designs that could assist you.

Marriage Mentors

We encourage congregations to invite people to become "marriage mentors" who lead groups of couples planning to marry or those recently married. Sharing this ministry among members of the congregation benefits both the couples and the marriage mentors. It also makes the idea of a more intensive process of marriage preparation or marriage enrichment more practical (especially if the congregation has a large number of weddings).

Marriage mentors often will build a relationship with the couple that can extend beyond their sessions together and support the couple during difficult times in the years ahead. In addition, marriage mentors can help integrate couples into the life of the congregation. Marriage is one time when people who do not ordinarily participate in the life of the church or who are new to the church arrive on the doorstep. We can welcome them by helping them build relationships with existing members, thus making it easier for them to come back to church after the wedding and become integrated into the life of the congregation. This experience may encourage those moving to other areas to turn to another congregation with the expectation of finding others "like that couple we worked with at St. Swithens."

An added benefit is that couples serving as marriage mentors often find their own marriages enriched by the experience of mentoring others. Even those who serve as education group leaders or married couples' retreat leaders usually find the experience helpful in their own marriages. In these days when marriages are buffeted by the winds and waves of many storms, congregations need to find ways to support people in their marriages. We hope that some of the ministries that grow out of this book will do that.

An area of ministry often overlooked is that of marriage enrichment. Maintaining and strengthening a healthy marriage takes work. Many couples will benefit from having the support of other couples and some type of regular meeting that encourages them to talk about their life together. This helps them affirm the good parts of their marriage and discover new ways of looking at and working with difficulties.

Marriage mentors often have more credibility (or a different kind of credibility) for couples than clergy. We recommend that the congregation's clergy meet with marriage mentors before they begin, in order to discuss perspectives and priorities and to provide training and support for their work. We have developed training programs that can help couples prepare to be marriage mentors or retreat leaders. (See the resource section.)

Developing Marriage Guidelines

We feel that there is some advance work that congregations should do if they are going to invite couples into a process that reflects the congregation's care and concern for them and their marriage. If a congregation has already done this work, the following may not be relevant. But if not, we encourage the clergy and vestry or other appointed group of the congregation to define some guidelines (but not unbending rules) for marriages conducted in a congregation. Ask this group to explore and understand for themselves:

- What is the sacramental nature of marriage?
- What is the role of the Christian community in a marriage?
- How is Christian marriage different from non-Christian marriage?
- How will we decide if we will celebrate a particular marriage? Under what circumstances will we say "no"? What canonical guidelines are we responsible for observing?
- How will we celebrate and support each marriage conducted in our congregation before, during, and after the ceremony?

By doing this work before a specific request arrives from a couple, the clergy and congregation avoid associating the guidelines with any specific individuals. It might be done by the clergy working with marriage mentors; it might also involve married couples and young adults who are not yet contemplating a marriage. The experience of exploring these questions could be an instructive adult education project for the congregation and may have a broader impact on the liturgy and life of the congregation as a whole, making the entire congregation aware of their role in supporting couples before, during, and after the wedding.

ᛒ For Clergy

This book will be useful in your premarital counseling sessions, either as the focus of each session or as supplemental reading. It might also be the basis of a premarital group, a married couples' group, an adult education program, or a married couples' retreat. You also may want to make the book available through the parish library or book table for couples to use on their own.

If you choose to use this book as part of your premarital sessions with each couple, you may want to ask couples to read between one and three chapters and discuss the questions with each other before meeting with you each time. You can then invite them to share their experience and use the questions to guide you in encouraging them to talk. If you are counseling couples where one or both partners are not resident locally, you can ask them to read the book and either meet with a clergyperson where they live or assemble a group to discuss it with them. Even a couple living in different locales can work through the book by phone or visits (or e-mail!). You could then arrange an occasional conference call to see how things are going and to help you decide if further work is needed.

It is also possible to work through this book in a weekend format (Friday night through Sunday afternoon). In this case, you can give couples about forty-five minutes to read each chapter and discuss the questions alone; then spend about forty-five minutes in a group discussion. You could also do it in a couple of Saturdays, although it would be difficult to discuss five chapters in a day unless the couples had already read the material and discussed their questions beforehand. Another plan might be to do one evening session at the beginning and another at the end with two Saturdays in between, each session reading and discussing four chapters. The advantage to a single weekend retreat is that you are more likely to be able to get all of the couples to attend at the same time. Split sessions inevitably result in someone missing one or more of the sessions.

If your congregation doesn't have many marriages in a given year, you may want to combine marriage preparation and marriage enrichment in one group. If you have a larger congregation and start a new group at least two or three times a year, the chances are likely that you can include several premarital couples. These groups don't have to be large; in fact, eight to ten people is probably the ideal size. One or two premarital couples, one marriage mentor couple, and one or two marriage enrichment couples is all you need.

We understand—only too well—that many couples are reluctant or "unable" to attend extensive premarital counseling sessions. However, we feel it is the church's responsibility to provide them with an opportunity to explore the issues raised in this book and, frankly, to insist that they do so. If you have been "settling for" one or two sessions with couples before a wedding, we hope that you will consider giving them this book and together identifying a way in which they can work with the material and be accountable to you for their work.

One difficult choice a couple preparing to marry needs to make is whether they will get married. The church can help couples who have little chance of maintaining a long-term healthy marriage choose to wait while they seek help in resolving difficult issues or even to decide not to marry. This help is especially important when abuse and/or active addiction is present in a relationship. The Christian community is called to participate in celebrating and blessing a union that is a sign of Christ's enduring love for us. When a relationship clearly is not such a sign but rather is destructive, the Christian community has a responsibility to intervene, provide support, refer to professionals, pray for healing, and offer such support as may be appropriate.

This book is not designed as a counseling book for those whose marriages are in serious trouble; therapy in those situations must be conducted by trained professionals. Most clergy do not have this type of training and should refer couples needing counseling to someone with those skills. This book can, however, be helpful for couples whose presenting complaint is vague—"Our marriage isn't what it used to be; we don't have any fun anymore; I don't know if we really love each other." In these cases reading and discussing the book may be a way for the couple to talk through what may be blocking the relationship and thus rekindle their love. It can also help pinpoint problems that might then be addressed in a counseling setting.

We understand the primary role of clergy to be one of reminding people of their vows made in marriage, of the power of God's love, and of the support of the Christian community. We believe that is best done by listening, asking open-ended or clarifying questions, loving both partners, and praying with and for the couple. Clergy can also offer the sacraments of the church, encouraging the couple to participate in the Eucharist, the Reconciliation of a Penitent, or the Laying on of Hands for Healing.

ONE

The Sacrament of Marriage

It signifies to us the mystery of the union between Christ and his Church
and Holy Scripture commends it to be honored among all people.
(BCP 423)

Christian marriage is a sacrament involving the whole Christian community. Christianity is a communal religion; we become Christians through baptism into the body of Christ, the church. In the church, marriage is called a symbol of the relationship of Christ to the church because of the enduring nature of Christ's love for us. The celebration and blessing of a marriage is an opportunity for the couple and the congregation to experience the joy of the promise of Christ's love for us. It provides an opportunity for the entire congregation to witness the exchange of vows and, as in the sacrament of baptism, it is an opportunity for those who are already married to renew their own marriage vows. For those not married, it is a reminder of the responsibility each of us has to support all those in our community who are married.

Of the sacraments of the church only one, matrimony, is specifically designed for two people. The other sacraments are generally received by an individual or, in the Eucharist, by an entire community. Only matrimony is administered for the benefit of two people and only in matrimony are two "recipients" required for the sacrament to be complete. Immediately we see something of the special nature of matrimony; it is meant to be shared by two people, but their sharing of matrimony becomes a symbol to us all of "Christ's union with his Church." That symbol is challenged when marriages fail at the current rate of almost fifty percent, with a significant cost to the individuals involved, to family life, and to society. This breakdown in marriages compels the church to reassess and reassert the role it plays in preparing the faithful for marriage and in supporting them in marriage.

In this context, the role of the congregation and the broader Christian community in the marriage relationship takes an entirely different meaning. The Christian community's support for the marriage must begin *before* the ceremony; it is expressed *during* the ceremony; and it continues *after* the service.

Before the Ceremony

It is important that congregations help those embarking on the marriage journey to prepare themselves for it, if the couple will accept and value this help. Couples considering marriage who have approached their clergyperson to perform the ceremony have already taken the first step in inviting the church to support their marriage. While they may have come to the clergyperson for very practical and not theological reasons (they need a minister and a church building), the opportunity is nevertheless presented. The challenge to the church community is to receive the couple, remembering the Christian symbolism their marriage embodies.

The Wedding at Cana

The story of the wedding at Cana (John 2:1-12) is often used to show that Jesus "instituted" (established) marriage as a sacrament. John describes the first week of Jesus' public ministry after his baptism. Jesus and his mother go to a wedding and the host runs out of wine during the feast afterwards. This would be humiliating to the couple and their families. So, at the urging of his mother, Jesus asks the servants to fill water jars with water and take them to the host, who discovers that the jars are filled with the finest wine. John says that this sign "revealed his glory" and led his disciples to believe in him.

What is your understanding of this passage? What does it mean to you to have Christ present at your wedding? One of the ways people have experienced Christ's presence is in the Eucharist. A "nuptial mass" (a wedding that includes a Eucharist) is becoming more popular as a way for the couple and their family and friends to experience Christ's presence in a real and tangible way.

If you are planning a wedding, what would having the Eucharist celebrated at your wedding mean to you? Often the couple presents the bread and wine at the offertory as a way of giving thanks to God for their love. Is this is something you want to do at your wedding?

When a couple makes a request to be married in the church, they can be invited to participate in a preparation process that involves them, the clergyperson who will officiate at the wedding, and members of the congregation. Church members who are serving as marriage mentors can lead groups or work with individual couples to help them prepare for their marriage and to support them in it.

This process assumes that both members of the couple are part of the congregation and that they are available for this preparation process before the wedding. Couples who work or are separated from each other or the congregation by distance may find participation in an ongoing process in the congregation difficult. We hope that congregations that have established a thorough preparation process as the norm will encourage couples to do this work in some other way.

There are many ways a congregation can support couples as they prepare for marriage. Often weddings happen privately and apart from the congregation. But many congregations include prayers for the couple in the intercessions at Sunday services several weeks before and immediately after the wedding. Some congregations include an invitation to the wedding in their Sunday bulletin and briefly describe the couples' post-wedding plans (will move here, go to school there, work in another town). These efforts help the congregation and couple connect with each other and build a support system that can help in the days ahead.

During the Ceremony

Beyond sharing in the preparation process, the Christian community is called to share in the ceremony itself. The wedding service is a public worship service and is open to all members of the congregation (the reception may be private). Attending the wedding of a couple in your congregation, even if you do not know them well, is one way to express support for that couple and their marriage. It also reminds us and them that we are accountable to each other and are called to support each other in good times and bad. During the ceremony we affirm that "we will" support the couple in their marriage when

---

Reaffirming Marriage Vows

While it is not included in the Episcopal/Anglican liturgies, we think it would be good if married couples attending a wedding were asked, "Do you reaffirm your commitment to love, honor, and cherish one another until you are parted by death?" much as we ask Christians attending a baptism to reaffirm their baptismal vows. This would reinforce the communal nature of the wedding service and the mutual accountability we have for one another. (If you choose to add this to a wedding service, we suggest it be asked just before the question requesting the congregation's support for the couple about to be married.)

we are asked: "Will all of you witnessing these promises do all in your power to uphold these two persons in their marriage?" (BCP 425). That affirmation is an important commitment for the days ahead.

After the Wedding

When we marry, we make our vows before God and the Christian community. We are accountable to God and to that community for keeping those vows. Our relationship and our actions have an impact that goes beyond just the two of us, even beyond our circle of family and friends. Our marriage has an impact on those who live in faithful community with us as Christians. The Christian community has a responsibility to care for those already married as much as it has for those seeking the church's blessing on their marriage.

Many congregations provide marital counseling in times of trouble but few provide ongoing support for those encountering all the normal ups and downs of marriage. Often the most helpful thing they can do is to provide opportunities for people to explore and discuss issues, listen to each other, and support each other in love and prayer.

&⁊　Civil and Sacramental Marriage

When we "get married" in a church ceremony, two things happen simultaneously. One is that we are married under civil law. A civil (nonreligious) marriage is conducted by a justice of the peace. It is a legal partnership. Each state or province defines the terms of that partnership differently, but there is an underlying legal agreement into which the partners enter.

> **Blessing of a Civil Marriage**
>
> Many couples who were married by a justice of the peace or in some other civil setting do not realize that the church offers *The Blessing of a Civil Marriage* (BCP 433). This service is a way for such couples to renew their vows before God and the church and to seek the blessing of God and the church on their marriage. It can be a simple part of a Sunday morning service, or it can be as elaborate as a traditional wedding.

That agreement specifies how their partnership will work. The most important aspects of that partnership govern property ownership and responsibility for each other and any children the couple may birth or adopt.

A clergyperson in the United States or Canada functions as a justice of the peace at a church wedding, thereby witnessing the formation of the legal partnership for the state or province. Simultaneously, the clergyperson and members of the congregation witness the exchange of the couple's vows to each other before God and participate in the sacramental rite (service or ceremony). In the Christian marriage service, the primary ministers of the wedding are the couple themselves—they give and receive the vows; the clergy and congregation are witnesses. Then together the entire community prays that God will help them fulfil the vows they have made. The clergyperson, as the person designated by the community to speak for them, leads the prayer that asks for and declares God's blessing on the couple. What makes Christian marriage unique, then, is that:

- a lifelong partnership is formed before God and the Christian community;
- God's blessing is sought and declared; and
- the marriage is an act that both proclaims and creates Christ's love in our love.

Another way to describe Christian marriage is that the couple's union *makes visible* God's grace and love for them and their love for each other while it also *gives* them the gift of God's grace and love. Their union is a sign of "the mystery of the union between Christ and his Church" to them and to the Christian community.

᎓ Marriage as a Sacrament

We have spoken of the marriage service as a sacrament. This implies that "the marriage" and "the sacrament" occur at some particular moment. This is simultaneously true and not true. We have also described marriage as a journey. It begins somewhere in the early stages of a relationship when a couple senses that their relationship is more than just friendship. At some point, the couple begins to talk about their relationship and how "right" it feels when they are together; they become aware of a dimension that is greater than the two of them. Usually they call that "love." They also may be aware of that love as a mystery—something intangible that is above and beyond them. That sense of mystery, that sense that their love is in some way holy, is what makes marriage a sacrament. The sacramental nature of marriage begins before the service and continues after the service. The wedding service is the time when the couple and the Christian community *celebrate* the

> *Marriage is a gift of God and a means of his grace, in which man and woman become one flesh. It is God's purpose that, as husband and wife give themselves to each other in love, they shall grow together and be united in that love, as Christ is united with his Church....*
>
> *In marriage, husband and wife give themselves to each other...they begin a new life together in the community. It is a way of life that all should reverence, and none should lightly undertake.* (BAS 528)

holiness of their love—the presence of Christ's love in their love—and seek God's *blessing* on their commitment to live and grow in that love.

The service is a sacramental moment, a time when the couple, in the presence of the community, proclaim that their love is graced by Christ's love and receive Christ's love as a blessing on their love. But the service is not the end of the sacrament. The journey continues and the presence of Christ's love in their lives continues even as their union continues to be a sign of Christ's love within the Christian community.

The presence and support of the Christian community in the years ahead help the couple to celebrate that love when they know it and to rediscover that love when it seems lost. The weekly gatherings of the eucharistic community and the more intimate gatherings of faithful Christians engaged in study, prayer, and ministry provide an environment where Christ's love is given and received. Christ's love is thus able to inflame the sometimes feeble embers of married love as couples rediscover that mystery of something greater than themselves.

In the wedding service the couple becomes a sign of God's love to the community. In the marriage journey, the community becomes a sign of God's love to the couple. Each has an important role to play in making God's love in Christ visible and real. So, it is important that the Christian community be involved in a couple's marriage and in their journey before and after the service. And it is important that the couple be involved in the Christian community, before and after the service.

You Don't Have to be Invited to Attend a Wedding

The Book of Alternative Services of the Anglican Church in Canada states:

> *Marriage is a public service of the Church. It should therefore be solemnized in the body of the Church (except for sufficient cause to the contrary) in the presence of the friends and neighbours of those who come to be married and of all the congregation of the Church. (BAS 526)*

Why do you think the entire congregation is encouraged to attend all weddings? How do you feel about attending a wedding in your church when you did not receive an invitation (which is technically an announcement and invitation to the reception)? Why would you attend? What would your role be?

ᙏ The Vocation of Marriage

Every Christian has a vocation, a primary way in which we embody and live out Christ's command to love God and love our neighbor and thus bring about the reign of God in our daily lives. When we choose to marry, we choose our partner as the nearest neighbor whom we will love most deeply and most fully. The marriage, therefore, is a vocation—the primary way in which the couple chooses to love God through loving each other.

When we promise to love our partner until we are parted by death, we make a lifelong commitment to do all in our power to help this person become who God created him or her to be—a lover of God and of neighbor. We also make a lifelong commitment to accept the help this person offers us as we grow to become who God created us to be. In this way our love for each other is a ministry (active service) and a vocation (a way of being).

Pre-nuptial Agreements

A pre-nuptial agreement is a legal contract between two people engaged to marry that defines how they will divide assets (and sometimes custody of children) should they divorce. It often is used in second marriages, especially when there are children from a previous marriage.

In a civil marriage (which is a partnership agreement) this might be a reasonable contract. But a Christian marriage calls you to make a lifelong commitment to each other—something that is difficult to do authentically if you have a ready-made agreement on how to end the marriage.

If you are contemplating a pre-nuptial agreement discuss the reasons for doing it with your clergyperson before you do so (lawyers and counselors do not necessarily use Christian principles in their counsel). If you can't trust your lives and fortunes to each other now, you may need to consider postponing or deciding against the marriage. If there are children from a previous relationship, you have a joint responsibility to provide for them by virtue of being "at one" with your spouse. A will and trust agreements provide ways for the two of you to ensure their financial well-being.

If you feel you must sign a pre-nuptial agreement, make sure that each partner has his or her own lawyer. Be especially cautious if the request to sign such an agreement comes right before the wedding. The embarrassment of cancelling a wedding is minor in comparison to the pain of later ending a marriage that may have been poisoned at its outset by a stance of "I love you but I don't trust you."

In the wedding service, the couple are the ministers of the marriage. The priest (or bishop) pronounces the church's blessing on the marriage, but the sacrament of marriage is administered by the couple. They say the vows that announce and create their lifelong commitment to love each other. As they are ministers of the marriage in the service, they continue to administer the sacrament to each other day after day. Again and again, new every day, they announce and create their lifelong commitment to love. The marriage journey moves us from *choosing to love* to *making a commitment to love* to *being and becoming a committed person, living and growing in love.* The married couple's growth in love and intimacy becomes their way to holiness, their life vocation.

QUESTIONS FOR COUPLES
TO DISCUSS

❧ **Marriage Preparation** *(for those preparing for marriage)*

- What first attracted you to your partner? What new dimensions have you discovered and come to appreciate about him or her?

- How do you feel when you are together—about yourself, your partner, and the two of you as a couple?

- What do you dislike or find uncomfortable about your partner? What do you identify as the areas of existing or potential differences, conflicts, or issues?

- If there are significant differences between you (age, race, ethnicity, cultural background, education), how do you feel about those differences? How do you think they will affect your marriage?

- How did you choose whether or not to live together before marriage? Why did you make that decision? How do you feel about it now?

- What led you to decide to marry? How did you make that decision? How do you feel about that decision now?

- What do you understand marriage to be? What do you think is the difference between Christian and non-Christian marriage? Why do you want to get married in the church?

- Who are the people who have supported you as individuals and as a couple? What do you believe is the Christian community's role in your marriage? What is your role in the Christian community?

- What does the Christian faith mean to you? Talk about your experience of God, Christ, and the church. If either or both of you have had a negative experience with religion, discuss how you might seek a positive experience of Christ's presence in your life.

- Do you expect to attend church after you are married? Will you attend separately or together? Where? How involved do you expect to be? If you plan to have children, what do you want them to find in a church? Do you expect that you will have a prayer life together as a couple and/or family?

- How do you anticipate spending religious and other holidays? What expectations do your families have about holidays, religion, participation in church and family events? How will you respond to their expectations?

- What does being a "minister of the marriage" mean to you? How is marriage a vocation? What is the difference between "making a commitment to love" and "becoming a committed person, living and growing in love?"

- What did you learn from this chapter? What decisions do you choose to make in response to what you learned?

‽ Marriage Enrichment *(for those already married)*

- What first attracted you to your spouse? What new dimensions have you discovered and come to appreciate about him or her since your marriage?

- What led you to decide to marry? How did you make that decision? How do you feel about that decision now? Why have you chosen to remain married?

- How do you feel when you are together—about yourself, your spouse, and the two of you as a couple? What would you like to change?

- What do you dislike or find uncomfortable about your spouse? Did you identify areas of existing or potential differences or conflict before your marriage? What areas have emerged since your marriage? How would you like to handle them?

- Who are the people who have supported you as individuals and as a couple? Has that support changed since your marriage? Is it adequate to meet your needs?

- What do you understand marriage to be? What do you think is the difference between Christian and non-Christian marriage? What do you believe is the Christian community's role in your marriage?

- How is marriage a vocation? What is the difference between "making a commitment to love" and "becoming a committed person, living and growing in love?" Where do you think you are on this continuum?

- What does the Christian faith mean to you? Talk about your experience of God, Christ, and the church. If either or both of you have had a negative experience of religion, discuss how you might seek a positive experience of Christ's presence in your life.

- Do you attend church? If so, do you attend separately or together? How involved are you? Are you comfortable with your current decisions about religion? If not, what would you change? If you have children, what sort of religious education do you want for them? Do you have a prayer life together as a couple and/or family?

- How do you spend religious and other holidays? What expectations do your families have about holidays, religion, and participation in church and family events? How have you responded to their expectations? Have you developed traditions of your own? Are you satisfied with the way you celebrate religious and other holidays? If not, spend some time discussing what changes you might make. Try to identify and develop traditions of your own, either adaptations of your childhood traditions or entirely new ones.

- What did you learn from this chapter? What decisions do you choose to make in response to what you learned?

QUESTIONS FOR GROUPS TO DISCUSS

- Introduce yourselves: Who are you? When, where, how did you meet? When, where, how did you get married or decide to get married? If you were married or plan to be married in the church, why did you decide to seek God's blessing on your marriage? (Note: if there are couples present who were not married in the church, group leaders may wish to comment that it is possible to have a civil marriage blessed and to ask the group to discuss why they think the church offers this opportunity.)

- Do you know or know about couples whose marriages you think are exceptional? What do you think makes their marriage exceptional? What do they do or what do you imagine they do to keep their marriage strong and healthy?

- What do you understand marriage to be? What do you think is the difference between Christian and non-Christian marriage?

- What do you believe is the Christian community's role in your marriage? What has been your role in the Christian community, before and after the wedding? Do you attend church? How involved are you? What difference do you think attending church has made or could make in your marriage?

- Where have you experienced God's presence in your relationship? What do you think a couple can do to make God's presence more real in their marriage?

- Consider this passage concerning marriage from the *Book of Common Prayer:* "It signifies to us the union between Christ and his Church and Holy Scripture commends it to be honored among all people." How do you think a marriage can signify the union between Christ and his church? Who is the "us" to whom this sign is given?

- How is marriage a vocation? What is the difference between "making a commitment to love" and "becoming a committed person, living and growing in love"?

- How do you respond to the idea of making a lifelong commitment?

- What do you think about pre-nuptial agreements? Do you think they affect a couple's ability to make and keep a lifelong commitment?

- What did you learn from this chapter? What decisions do you choose to make in response to what you learned?

S U G G E S T E D   P R O J E C T S

- Make lists of major holidays and describe how your family celebrated them in the past and how you spend them now or think you will spend them in your marriage (what you eat, how you decorate the home, whose family you visit). Share your lists with each other and discuss any differences in how your families spent holidays and how you expect to spend them now.

- If you are members of different denominations or faiths, attend services at each other's house of worship; observe and then discuss the differences and similarities.

- Think of one meaningful religious tradition you would like to have as a part of your home or worship life. Spend some time thinking about what meant a lot to you as a child, observing what others do, and pondering what is meaningful to you today. It might be something as simple as grace before meals. Or it might be attending worship together, studying the scriptures together, or listening to music that puts you in touch with the sacred. It might even be finding and hanging artwork that has sacred meaning for you. Whatever it is, pick at least two things you can do as a couple that brings you closer to God.

- Discuss and identify activities you do that help you experience your marriage as a sacrament and vocation. Identify at least two things you would like to do.

Extended Families

Dearly beloved: We have come together in the presence of God to witness and bless....
(BCP 423)

As children we learned about marriage by watching the adults around us. The more significant the adult, the more he or she taught us. So, most people learned how to "be married" from their parents or primary caregivers. If your parents' marriage was good, you are likely to have learned good ways of being together. If one or both you experienced your parents' marriage as less than ideal or perhaps even destructive, then you will tend to repeat those patterns unless you consciously practice new ways of being together. Many people *swear* they will never be like their parents and yet, despite their best intentions, often find themselves acting in those same ways. This is why many people in the middle of an argument with their spouse or while disciplining their child suddenly realize that they sound "just like mom" or "just like dad."

Because of this, it is extremely important that you understand your families' values and how members of your families relate to each other. Obviously, it is best if you can spend time with each other's families. If that is not possible, tell stories about how your parents interacted with each other and how their interactions affected you. Recognize that you have integrated some of your parents' ways of thinking and acting into your own personality. Try to see where you think and act like them. The more you pretend that you are not like your parents, the more likely you are to repeat the very patterns you hope to avoid. It is only when you *recognize* the behaviors that you have a choice about whether to continue them or change. Once you are aware of behaviors and patterns you want to change, you can then adopt new behaviors by practicing them until they become automatic.

✌ Problematic Family Interactions

Patterns of behavior in your family of origin that are destructive or hurtful have the potential to harm your marriage. Physical, sexual, or emotional abuse, alcohol or drug abuse, excessive dependence, passivity or dominance, workaholism, perfectionism, or "living apart but in the same house" are all patterns that can have a negative impact on your marriage, and it is naive to assume that you will somehow escape their effects. If the negative patterns are already evident in your relationship you may want to rethink getting married, at least at this time. Recognize that anyone who has experienced a seriously negative childhood will generally need assistance in building a positive adult life. Occasionally miracles do happen—but usually help is needed!

It is tempting to be complacent and assume that somehow you can "muddle through" the effects of serious family problems. Dysfunctional family patterns of any sort require understanding and conscious action to prevent the pattern from repeating itself in your relationship and subtly undermining your marriage. You will need to enter the relationship with the clear understanding that extra effort will be required from both of you, probably throughout your marriage. This is not to say that one should never enter a marriage with someone from a family where there are serious problems. If that were true, there wouldn't be many marriages! Rather, we are encouraging you to be realistic about what challenges you are likely to encounter and plan for how you will handle them when they arise.

> *Therefore a man leaves his father and his mother and clings to his wife, and they become one flesh.* (Genesis 2:24)
>
> Before joining with each other, each partner must "leave" his or her family, and the families must "give up" the family member so he or she can enter into the marriage relationship fully. Traditionally this letting go has been symbolized in the marriage ceremony by the father "giving away" the bride. This tradition is based in the social reality that women had no legal standing; a father "owned" his daughter and the marriage transferred ownership to the husband. Today many couples have all members of both immediate families respond to the question, "Who presents this woman and this man to be married to each other?" (BCP 437). The Canadian *Book of Alternative Services* asks: "Do you, members of the families of N. and N., give your blessing to this marriage?" (BAS 531).

Couples who are already married also need to look at family relationships and see how these patterns have affected their own relationship. Often couples who are a few years into a marriage can understand and resolve their difficulties by looking at their families and the differences between them.

If one or both of you have been married and the previous spouse is alive, it is important that you discuss and resolve any issues concerning that relationship or relationship with his or her family. What contact is there? What contact do you expect there to be? Is the prior marital relationship sufficiently "disentangled," or will emotional attachments create problems in this new marriage? It is important that divorced spouses have enough time and distance from their previous spouse to create space for a new relationship. Frequent, involved interactions with a former spouse may suggest an unreadiness for a new marriage.

> "In marriage, husband and wife...are linked to each other's families."
> (BAS 528)

If there are children from a previous marriage, it is important that the previous family unit work out issues of custody, visitation, child support, and the like before either person enters a new marriage. When a new marriage is formed, there must be clarity about obligations and expectations regarding children, time, and money. The parent may wish to establish a will and/or trust fund to provide for the care of children prior to another marriage. If so, it is helpful to discuss such arrangements with your future spouse and to make appropriate arrangements regarding future joint assets.

If a previously married spouse has close relationships with former in-laws that he or she wishes to maintain, include the current spouse in those relationships, either directly, if so desired, or indirectly. Make sure you don't act as if he or she doesn't exist (going alone for visits, never mentioning your partner's name). Discuss the ways any relationships with former relatives affects your current marriage and make adjustments as needed to support it.

It is important to recognize that you marry more than an individual; you marry "into" that person's family. Not only will past relationships have an effect, but current relationships will also affect your marriage. Healthy family relationships often strengthen and enhance a couple's relationship and provide invaluable support in times of trouble. Unhealthy family relationships can cause difficulties and undermine a relationship.

Families can have very different expectations about the level of involvement in each other's lives, about values and lifestyles, and about expectations for personal and emotional support. The first step is to identify any differences between your own values and expectations. The level of involvement issue often emerges in planning the wedding (who is involved in making which decisions).

The next major issue often arises when the first holidays come and both families expect you to be with them. Or the question arises around how many visits (or phone calls), initiated by whom and sharing how much information. Blended marriages with one or more sets of step-children and the attendant step-relatives add another degree of complexity.

❧ Developing Helpful Family Interactions

It is important for the two of you to decide what patterns of family interaction are most supportive to you and your marriage. While that may sound selfish, the reality is that you will not be able to be effective as parents or supportive to your family members if you do not nurture your primary relationship with each other. Obviously, you will need to care for any children you might already have—but not at the expense of your relationship. And you probably will want to find ways of relating to other family members on some regular basis—but not at the expense of your own relationship.

You must discuss and decide what will work for you and then support each other in making that decision known to others. So, for example, if one family's expectation is that you will spend every Sunday evening with them and the two of you decide that that is too frequent, you need to say "no" even if other family members become upset. You do not need an excuse or explanation, but you do need to present it as a joint decision. You might simply say, "We have decided that we are not able to be with

---

Extending Your Family

When you marry, you have the opportunity to extend your family relationship to include others. Sometimes your new in-laws become closer to you than your own relatives. In the biblical story of Ruth and Naomi, Naomi, the mother-in-law, lives with her two sons until they both die. Then she returns to her relatives and encourages her daughters-in-law to do the same. One does so, but the other, Ruth, does not. She chooses to stay with her mother-in-law, saying:

Do not press me to leave you or to turn back from following you! Where you go, I will go; where you lodge, I will lodge; your people shall be my people, and your God my God. Where you die, I will die—there I will be buried. May the Lord do thus and so to me, and more as well, if even death parts me from you! (Ruth 1:16-17)

This passionate pledge of loyalty, trust, and commitment is often used as a musical selection at a wedding. While it is appropriate there, it also speaks to the connections we may make with our spouse's family.

you every week. We would like to visit [once a month]." Resist getting drawn into protests and negotiations. Just explain that "we have discussed it and decided that this is best for us at this time."

The point is to resist being pressured into doing something that does not support you as a couple or, even worse, is a significant drain on your relationship. When a couple does what "the family" wants, it may mean that the spouse involved has not adequately separated from his or her family and/or that there is some serious family difficulty. Failing to establish the boundary between your family unit and your extended family may create confusion and problems.

One way to gain clarity about this is to remember that no one else can take responsibility for the well-being of your relationship. If you sacrifice that in order to take care of the needs of others (even if they are real and "valid"), you will damage or even lose your marital relationship and usually your ability to respond effectively to others' needs. It is a matter of proportion and priority. Most of us have others who want or need us in their lives—parents, children, other relatives and friends. And it is right and good to respond to those needs. However, when we enter a marriage relationship, everything changes. That relationship becomes primary and the needs of others become secondary. That reality may be difficult for all involved. But it is essential if the marriage relationship is to survive and thrive. Eventually everyone will learn that if the couple nurtures their relationship, they will generally have enough energy to nurture other relationships as well. Meanwhile, others in the family probably will have expanded their network of people and resources to help them get what they need.

> *Jesus said: "For this reason a man shall leave his father and mother and be joined to his wife, and the two shall become one flesh. So they are no longer two, but one flesh.* (Mark 10:7-8)
>
> What does this passage say about the change in familial relationships that occurs when one marries? What constitutes "leaving" your parents? What feeling do you think this creates for parents who have loved and nurtured their child? What are ways one can respect those feelings and still "leave" one's parents?

One important rule to remember is that you cannot change the behaviors of others; you can only change your own. You cannot make others happy; they are responsible for their own happiness. The two of you are committing to working together to build a relationship of love that will nurture and support each other. Your respective families can help you or they can hinder you in doing that. But you choose whether to accept help when it is offered or to allow that which hinders. Discussing what helps and hinders your relationship will go a long ways toward helping you decide when, where, and how you will relate to your families.

ɞ Rejection by One or Both Families

Sometimes one or both families (or members of a family) may reject your partner. When this happens it is important to try to understand the reasons. If your family is fairly "healthy" and normally "reasonable," consider their objections seriously (especially if they are from more than one family member). Sometimes, in the midst of "falling in love" we are unable to see that which is obvious to others who know us and love us.

Familial objection often signals that there really is a problem; the question is how to respond. While it is helpful to discuss the concerns with family members, it is best to seek the support of an objective person, preferably a professional who can help you sort through the questions raised by the rejection. The purpose of such discussion is:

- to decide if the objections raise valid concerns you wish to address;
- if so, to identify how you will address them; or, if not, to identify the consequences of proceeding with the marriage; and
- to decide how to relate to those who object.

ɞ Dealing with Differences

Sometimes family and friends may object to your marriage because your partner is significantly different from you in some way: background, wealth, race, religion, education, and so on. This often creates conflict that may result in alienation. While we ourselves were fortunate in finding our inter-racial marriage accepted by our families, we did encounter rejection from acquaintances and co-workers. We needed to talk as a couple about how to respond to that rejection.

It is possible that the differences between the two of you make others uncomfortable. That may be their problem, but it may also point to something you need to examine. Accepting people's negative reaction as useful information can be helpful. We suggest the following way of dealing with objections to the differences between you:

- Understand the impact this difference between you *will have* on your marriage. If you are young or inexperienced, talk with one or more couples with similar differences about their experience.

- Assess your ability to handle rejection. If one of you is so upset by being rejected that it affects his or her work, sleep, or general well-being, seek professional help or reconsider the marriage. On the other hand, if you assume people's discomfort with your "mixed marriage" is their problem or are not concerned about their discomfort, you may lose a few relationships but it is not likely to significantly hurt your marriage.

- Respond calmly. Once you understand the potential impact and have assessed your ability to handle it, don't let others get you into arguments about it. Calmly state that you understand their concern for you but you have assessed the situation and decided that you can and will handle it appropriately.

- Build a united front and support each other. Major differences between two people (especially if they are visible) create a reaction and affect your relationship. You can't do anything about how others feel or react, but you can find ways to support each other and deflect others' rejection. Once you are married, your job is to defend

---

In-law Troubles

What do you do if you can't stand your future in-laws and can already see trouble on the horizon or, if already married, you're deep into in-law problems? First, be honest with each other and talk about how you will handle this difficulty. If at all possible, it is important to develop a positive or at least neutral relationship with your in-laws, even if that requires much tolerance and patience on your side. Remember, these people raised the person you love, so they can't be all bad! And your spouse has a responsibility, if not a desire, to be in relationship with his or her parents and family.

If your in-laws engage in some behaviors that make you uncomfortable or offend you, you may need to adopt defensive strategies. If you and your spouse have tried discussing the situation (or decided that discussion would be fruitless), it may be best just to ignore the behavior. You can calmly state that you will not listen to or participate in such behavior and leave the room whenever it occurs. Or you can just pretend it didn't happen. Offensive language and behaviors are often continued when they provoke a reaction and may stop when the desired reaction isn't forthcoming.

Finally, you and your spouse may decide to limit your interactions with this family member. If this is necessary, try to check in every so often...people do change!

your relationship against friends and relatives who might continue to protest and try to undermine it. If necessary, limit your contact with those who choose to make this an ongoing issue.

Different Denominations, Different Faiths

If the two of you belong to different Christian denominations, you will need to discuss which church to attend, which holidays to keep, and how you will teach your children. If one partner is a member of another faith group (Jewish, Islamic, or Buddhist, for example) or if one partner has no faith affiliation, then it becomes even more important to explore faith issues fully. Interfaith couples need to decide whether they will maintain two faiths or if one partner will switch. You need to address whether children will be raised in one faith or both. You need to discuss holiday and family expectations fully and agree upon a plan.

It is most important that each partner respect and not denigrate the other's beliefs and that children are not given contradictory information. It is also important that the couple be united in how they will deal with family members who may pressure them in various ways. Whether you maintain both faiths or choose one, it is important for both partners to understand the values and traditions of each other's faith, to identify what is meaningful to each partner and what, in your partner's faith, is meaningful to you. If possible, identify what values and traditions you can share in your new life together.

❧ Broadening Family Relationships

Marriage provides an opportunity to establish different and new family relationships. Your relationship with your own family members will change. Family relationships with your in-laws will develop. Your relationships with others in society and your place in the Christian community will probably change as well. Your new marriage will need all the support it can get to thrive in today's rough and tumble world. Don't be afraid to ask for the support you need. Families can help, and you may be surprised by the value of their support and their willingness to give it. Sibling relationships often become more important over time, especially when parents develop health problems or die and your siblings become your primary "next of kin."

Your Christian community can help, too. Again, don't be afraid to ask for what you need. Wherever you go, you can find congregations of Christians gathered to worship and support each other. These communities have a responsibility to support you in your marriage. You can find experienced couples who can be mentors or take on "grandparent" roles with your children. You can find others who can become extended family for you, especially if your own families live far from you. Many congregations have various groups that help you get to know people and find those with whom you want to become friends. Some have classes that can strengthen your marital relationship or parenting skills.

Most congregations have a clergyperson and/or trained lay person who can offer pastoral care or, if needed, will help you find a professional counselor. They will be compassionate listeners who support you in love and prayer while you work out minor difficulties or while you gather the courage to tackle tough issues with a professional counselor. Often they will meet with you for several sessions and then refer you to a counselor if you need additional help. Prayer, love, and just discussing things in the presence of a neutral, compassionate listener who asks guiding questions can go a long way toward helping you resolve your problems. If that isn't adequate, seek the help of a professional counselor and ask those in the Christian community to continue to support you in prayer.

At each wedding the priest asks those present to make a commitment to the couple: "Will all of you witnessing these promises do all in your power to uphold these two persons in their marriage?" The Christians present at the wedding answer "We will" on behalf of all Christians. This means that every congregation anywhere in the world has a responsibility to help you live a truly Christian marriage. That is a gift to you; all you need to do to receive it is turn to them for their help in times of trouble. You and the church are bound together by virtue of your choosing to be married in the church, and of the church choosing to witness and bless your marriage.

QUESTIONS FOR COUPLES
TO DISCUSS

⅋ Marriage Preparation

- How did your parents (and/or other significant adults in your childhood) relate to each other? What about their relationship did you especially like? especially dislike?

- What was the effect of their relationship on you as a child? Did you make any decisions about wanting to "be like" or "NOT be like" them? Why or why not?

- In what ways are you like your mother? father? other significant adults who helped raise you? siblings? What effect do you think they will have on your marriage?

- What are your current familial relationships? Are there any particularly close relationships? estranged relationships? Describe them. How are they likely to affect your marriage?

- How do you relate to your partner's family? How do your family members relate to your partner? Are there any significant differences or disagreements between you and your partner's family or your partner and your family that may cause difficulties? Do you see any patterns in how family members relate to other in-laws? How are any of these likely to affect your marriage?

- Do you anticipate that one or both families will interfere in your decisions about how to live, manage your household, raise your children? If so, how will you handle that?

- Do you anticipate caring for parents or other relatives in their old age or illness? Do you plan to have them live with you? How do you think your marriage might be changed by this?

- What are benefits you anticipate you will receive from your relationship with your partner's family? What benefits might your partner receive from his or her relationship with your family?

- What do you value most about the relationship you and your partner have with your families?

- What did you learn from this chapter? If these questions raised any concerns, what do you want to do about them?

Marriage Enrichment

- How did your parents (and/or other significant adults in your childhood) relate to each other? What about their relationship did you especially like? especially dislike?

- What was the effect of their relationship on you as a child? Did you make any decisions about wanting to "be like" or "NOT be like" them? Why or why not?

- In what ways are you like your mother? father? other significant adults who helped raise you? siblings? What effect do you think they have had on your marriage?

- What are your current familial relationships? Are there any particularly close relationships? estranged relationships? Describe them. How have those relationships affected your marriage?

- How do your family members relate to each of you? How do you relate to your spouse's family members? Are there any significant differences or disagreements? Do you see any patterns in how your family members relate to other in-laws? How have these changed your marriage? What would you like to change?

- Do any relatives live with you? Do you anticipate them living with you in their old age or illness? How does that/might that affect your marriage?

- What are some of the benefits you receive from your relationship with your spouse's family? What benefits might your spouse receive from his or her relationship with your family?

- What do you value most about the relationship you and your spouse have with your families? What do you think you could do to strengthen relationships with your family or your spouse's family?

- What did you learn from this chapter? If these questions raised any concerns, what do you want to do about them?

QUESTIONS FOR GROUPS TO DISCUSS

- Describe "bad marriages" you know or have seen portrayed in the media. What do you think makes them bad marriages? What helped create and sustain them as such? What actions could a couple in a bad marriage take to help change that situation?

- What childhood story comes to your mind when you think about marriage? Explore that story. How do you think it has influenced your attitudes, behaviors, or values in your relationship?

- How did you experience marriage through your parents' marriage and those of other significant adults in your childhood? How do you think that has affected your relationship?

- What is your family's history of involvement with each other (visits, advice, lending money, etc.)? What has been your relationship with your families? What have you learned about each other's families that surprised you? pleased you? discouraged you? Discuss ways you might respond to some of the issues identified by the group.

- What are examples of difficulties with parents, siblings, or in-laws? What can a couple do to respond to those difficulties?

- Do any relatives live with you? Do you anticipate them living with you in their old age or illness? What are some of the issues a couple might face in these situations?

- What are some of the benefits you receive from your relationship with your partner's family? What benefits might you receive from his or her relationship with your family?

- What do you value most about the relationships you have with your families? What do you think you could do to strengthen those relationships?

- Consider this quotation from the *Book of Common Prayer:* "Dearly beloved: We have come together in the presence of God to witness and bless...."). What does it mean for families "to witness and bless" a couple's marriage? Who does the blessing? Do you feel this happened/will happen at your wedding? What difference do you think it has made/will make in your marriage?

- What did you learn from this chapter and discussion? Is there anything you plan to do because of what you learned?

S U G G E S T E D   P R O J E C T S

- Visit or recall a recent visit to each partner's family of origin and describe what you observed or remember observing. (If a visit is not possible, imagine a specific situation, such as a family meal.) Compare and contrast family habits, styles, values. Identify those you already have or that you especially want to "adopt" or "reject" in your life together.

- Develop a family tree that goes back at least three or four generations. Identify stories about the marriage of each family member, paying special attention to how they related to each other, parents, siblings, children, and in-laws. Are there any patterns that emerge? Family patterns tend to get passed along from one generation to the next. Do you see any evidence of that in your relationship? Discuss how you might handle any pattern you see that you do not wish to repeat.

THREE

Being with Others

...that each may be to the other a strength in need, a counselor
in perplexity, a comfort in sorrow, and a companion in joy.
(BCP 429)

During the time before and shortly the wedding, most couples are closer to each other than anyone else. Often prior relationships fade as this most important one comes into the foreground. Hobbies, school, family, and work take a secondary place in our lives; we naturally want to spend as much time with our loved one as we can.

This is an important time of bonding. As we draw closer to each other, we tell many of our life stories, recounting the times of pain and shame as well as the highlights and glories. Most of us talk about all the ups and downs we encounter on a day-to-day basis, enjoying the fact that we have someone who will share our burdens and joys. All of this is natural and appropriate. The difficulties arise when the bonding is either incomplete or too strong.

Some couples do not have this time of bonding, either before or after the wedding. Their courtship may be very fast or the relationship may stay on a superficial level. The life stories are never told, or they are disguised or misrepresented. The daily hurts and joys are never shared or only mentioned in passing. The bonding between the couple is incomplete.

With other couples, only one of the partners is willing and able to build an intimate relationship. In this case, one person may tell life stories, both past and present, but the other partner may not really listen or may even discount the stories, dismissing them as "unimportant" or encouraging the person to "forget about it," to "stop getting so upset," or otherwise discouraging this type of conversation. Usually this pattern is marked by the absence of any true sharing on that partner's side.

If either of these patterns is true of your relationship, pay attention. Either more time is needed for you to develop and deepen the relationship, or one (or both) partners may need professional assistance to overcome emotional or relational difficulties. Whatever the cause, it is not realistic to assume that things will magically change by themselves. A marriage relationship needs to be built on a strong foundation of communication and trust. Each of you needs to be able to share both pain and joy and to experience your partner's support and love.

Sometimes the opposite happens and the time of bonding is so intense that everyone and everything else is shut out. As long as it is only for a short time, this intensity may not be a problem. But when one's partner is the sole source of support and companionship, difficulties will arise. No single person can meet all of our needs. Asking your partner to be the only person who can listen, support, and affirm you places an undue burden on your partner and your relationship. While the intensity of your relationship may be appealing for a while, eventually the overdose of closeness will suffocate the relationship. Your primary relationship needs to be *primary* without becoming your *only* relationship.

A simple way to begin working on developing healthy interdependence is for each person to develop at least one pleasurable activity done without the other. It might be a sport or exercise program or hobby—anything that allows each partner to have a separate identity and to build relationships with others who can provide support and companionship. These less intimate relationships may be social friends, colleagues who occasionally go out together after work, a sports partner, or members of a group dedicated to a similar cause. These "other relationships" often include one's family members and friends from years before.

Women are from Venus, Men are from Mars

Author John Gray points out that men and women often have different needs for closeness and distance. Men often seek "space" after a time of intimacy by distancing themselves from those they are close to. Women often seek intimacy by talking about issues and wanting their partner to listen to them. The tendency men have to fix problems and propose solutions (rather than just listening and assuming she can fix it herself) short-circuits the intimacy women are seeking. On the other hand, women's pursuit of men when they withdraw short-circuits their ability to reconnect. While Gray's theory may be overly simplistic, it is helpful to remember it when closeness and distance become an issue in your relationship.

Members of your Christian community can become close friends and valued supporters in both good times and bad.

Excessive dependency on each other for support and companionship calls for a serious examination of your relationship before getting married. If you are already married, it is important to address this issue promptly before it undermines your relationship.

A healthy marital relationship maintains a balance between self and the couple, between the relationship of the two partners and relationships with others. It moves back and forth between closeness and distance. Failure to create enough distance or "space" in the relationship often leads to fights, as the partner in need of it literally fights to get it. Failure to create enough closeness in the relationship often leads to a slow, quiet death as the two partners gradually drift apart. Some of the ongoing work one does in a marriage is the work of maintaining this balance of distance and closeness.

⅋ Inappropriate Relationships with Others

An imbalance in one's primary relationship often manifests itself by one partner (or even both) becoming involved in a competing relationship with someone else. The lonely person, feeling cut off from his or her partner, can suddenly "fall in love" with someone who is ready and willing to build an intimate relationship. Likewise, the partner who is suffocating in a relationship may seek "air" by turning to someone else. Often these relationships do not start as sexual relationships. Rather, they begin as personal relationships, meeting intimacy needs. Sexual overtones and perhaps actions may arise later.

The first question to ask yourself when you are sexually or emotionally attracted to another person is: "How do I feel about my partner and our relationship?" If you are building another relationship that is becoming emotionally and/or sexually intimate, the chances are highly likely that your primary relationship is suffering some type of imbalance. The first thing to do is to distance yourself from your new relationship and pay attention to reestablishing balance in your marriage. After that, you will be able to establish other relationships that are more appropriate.

It is important for you to discuss what each of you considers appropriate boundaries in relationships with others. By boundaries we mean those unspoken, unwritten "lines" in relationships that tell us what level of physical, sexual, or emotional intimacy is appropriate. Some people's boundaries are so high that they rarely, if ever, form intimate relationships outside their marital or family relationships. Other people's boundaries are so low that they will discuss intimate things with almost anyone and may accept or initiate inappropriate forms of intimacy. Most of us fall somewhere in between.

Most couples negotiate what feels "right" to them—how much talking about "our business," how much touching, how much time spent with others and under what circumstances, is acceptable. When one partner does something the other partner considers too intimate, he or she "gets jealous" and a discussion, if not a fight, may result. Partners with very different boundaries can spend a great deal of time in conflict until they begin either to adjust their boundaries or to adapt to each other's differences. But those differences can also be helpful, especially if one's boundary levels are causing problems. For example, a partner with high boundaries can help a partner with low boundaries say "no" to unwanted intimacy, while a partner with low boundaries can help a partner with high boundaries risk building new relationships.

While we usually think of infidelity as sexual or intense emotional involvement with others, there is another dimension to infidelity. The marital relationship is a relationship of trust and faithfulness. As we build that relationship over time, we gain information about each other that is not entrusted to others. To use that information against your partner or betray your partner by talking about it to someone else is to be unfaithful. So, too, is making fun of or putting down your partner in public. These behaviors betray the trust your partner has placed in you and they violate the vow you made to love, cherish, and remain faithful to your partner. The damage these types of infidelity cause to your marital

Extramarital Affairs

If yours is a remarriage where one or both of you or a previous spouse have had an affair, it is important that you discuss what happened and your feelings about it with your current partner. If your previous spouse had the affair, talk about why you believe it happened, how you handled it, what you learned, what you would do differently next time. If either of you has been in an affair, identify what made you vulnerable and pay special attention to addressing that area of your life. Talk about the signs and work out, in advance, what you will do when you see any signs of trouble. Use your previous problem as a positive force to strengthen this marriage.

If you are currently engaged in an affair or are becoming emotionally or sexually involved with someone other than your partner, stop immediately and seek help from a counselor and/or your clergyperson. You will need to identify the personal and marital problems that have led you to this point, but you cannot do so while you are involved in the relationship.

relationship are every bit as serious as that caused by sexual infidelity. Both undermine and destroy your marriage.

❧ Relationships with Others

Developing good social relationships with others is important, beyond helping to maintain a balance in your marriage. Good friends are enjoyable, can give you an honest perspective on yourself and decisions you need to make, and support you in the difficult times. Choose your friends with care. Remember, some of what people are rubs off on you when you spend time with them. Think about who you want to become and choose to spend time with people who have those values, characteristics, and skills. If you simply live for the moment, socializing with whomever comes along and doing whatever they suggest, you may soon find yourself going down a path you do not like. Or you may stagnate and find yourself, twenty years from now, regretting that you never challenged yourself to grow and expand your horizons. The friends you choose can help you do that.

Each of you should develop at least one relationship that challenges you. It may be someone whose skill at a sport exceeds yours, or who has personal qualities you admire. Or it may be someone involved in a social activity you wouldn't naturally

---

King David's Adultery

We often think of biblical heroes as people who lived especially saintly lives. It turns out that many of them are as human as the rest of us. Read the story of David's adultery told in 2 Samuel 11. From the roof of his palace David sees a beautiful woman named Bathsheba, the wife of one of his soldiers at war. David summons Bathsheba to the palace and has intercourse with her. She gets pregnant, so David summons her husband, Uriah, home from the fields of battle, hoping he'll have sex with his wife and believe the child is his. When Uriah refrains, David sends him to the front lines and directs the rest of the army to desert him so Uriah would be killed in battle. David then took Bathsheba as his wife.

When David is later called to account for his actions by the prophet Nathan, he repents. One of the consequences of his actions is that the child conceived in adultery dies. Later he and Bathsheba have a second child, Solomon, who becomes a wise and wealthy king.

Our actions have consequences. What are some of the consequences of adultery or of "crossing the line" in relationships in today's world? What does David's story tell us about how we might respond to being called to account for our actions?

join, or committed to a cause you want to learn about. Choose to nourish and build those relationships. The two of you will find yourself gaining skills and growing more like your friends.

Finally, as a couple you need to develop friendships with wise and trustworthy individuals or couples who can be there for you in time of need. The day may well come when your life will fall apart: one of you may be diagnosed with cancer, your child may die, your sibling may commit suicide, your home may burn down. Whatever it is, you will need friends you can turn to. Usually they will be people of faith who can and will walk with you through the difficult times. Throughout your life look for these people and stay in touch with them. When the difficult times come, the two of you will have friends to support you. If you don't have such people in your life when trouble strikes, your local congregation is a good place to turn. The clergy can support you and can help you find others who are willing and able to stand by you.

Dealing with the "Isms"

If you face racism, sexism, or any other oppression in today's society, building supportive relationships becomes even more important. Usually these relationships will be with people "like you" because others generally cannot really understand or empathize with what you face. These same-group relationships are important, even if others imply you shouldn't want or need them. Build the relationships that help you deal with the "isms" you face.

Sometimes one of you will face an "ism" not faced by the other; in our case, Linda does not face the racism Del encounters daily. Discuss the support each of you needs, and recognize that you cannot provide all the necessary support for each other. When you are a couple, the "ism" faced by one partner will affect both of you, so you may want to seek support as a couple as well as looking for individual support.

❧ Getting Help from a Counselor

Sometimes a couple develops difficulties that are so serious that their own discussions, the support of friends, and the help of clergy are not enough. At this point it becomes important to seek help from a professional counselor, preferably someone with experience in marital counseling. There are several reasons why people seek marital counseling:

- they have decided to leave the relationship or marriage and want the counselor to validate their decision;

- they don't know what they want to do and expect the counselor to decide for them;
- they want the relationship to work but expect the counselor to "fix it" (in other words, they don't want to face the issues or do the work necessary to heal the relationship); or
- they want the relationship to work, are willing to do the necessary work, and look to the counselor to help them.

A competent counselor can and will help you do only the last item. A counselor can help you implement your decision or can help you decide what to do, but cannot make your decision or do your work for you.

Before you select a counselor to help you, know what you want and need from that person, make sure the counselor is certified and qualified, and find out how committed he or she is to building up your marital relationship. Some counselors focus on helping each of you identify your individual needs and how to get them met, even if that is outside of your marriage. Others may focus on helping you resolve the conflict in your marriage by ending the marriage. If you approach counseling with the goal of strengthening your marital relationship, counselors often can help you do that if they are committed to that goal and competent in their work.

Ask a friend, clergyperson, or member of your congregation to recommend someone they know. Your company may also have an employee assistance program that can recommend someone. Pick a person, make an appointment, and tell them what you want and need. Try it for awhile. If it doesn't seem to be working or it doesn't "feel right," try someone else. This is not to encourage you to avoid dealing with painful issues by switching counselors; rather, it is to say that you are in charge and you need to be clear about what help you expect the counselor to provide. Of course, you also need to be willing to do the work required to resolve the issues that brought you to the counselor in the first place. Your willingness to work and the help of a competent professional can save many marriages that might otherwise die.

People are slowly coming to the realization that the enormous costs of divorce to the couple, their children, families, and friends make it important to work at renewing existing relationships. The vast majority of marriages are worth trying to put back together. Within the Christian context, it is helpful to remember that the vows taken are sacred vows—a commitment made in God's presence and with God's blessing. One should neither make nor break such a commitment lightly.

Finally, we encourage you to seek the support of clergy and other lay people in your congregation even if you are seeing a professional counselor. Their love and prayers can give you the support you need to work out your difficulties.

&ba; The Sacred Vows of Marriage

The promises you make in the wedding service are sacred. You make a personal commitment to each other in the presence of God, who becomes a part of that commitment. These vows are vows of trust that you will be faithful and true to each other above all else. When that trust is broken, serious harm is done to your partner, to yourself, and to your relationship. Harm is also done to the Christian community because when that trust is broken, the Body of Christ is broken. Our individual actions have an impact far beyond ourselves: this is what makes emotional and sexual affairs so damaging. It is not a question of being discovered or breaking the rules; rather, breaking the basic trust relationship in a marriage creates broken relationships, and that brokenness has consequences. Those consequences may be different for each of us, but they are real and they are painful.

> ### Being Faithful
>
> *Will you love her [him],...and, forsaking all others, be faithful to her [him] as long as you both shall live?* (BCP 424)
>
> What constitutes "forsaking all others" or "being faithful"? Who decides whether I am or am not faithful? What difference does it make?

As Christians we are called to be in relationship with God and each other in Christ (BCP 855). Those relationships "in Christ" are sacred. When we break those relationships we are called to acknowledge our fault and seek each other's forgiveness and God's forgiveness. While a Christian partner is called to forgive, it is not always easy to do so. Often God's love, working in and through us, is the power that enables the wounded partner to forgive. The fact that God is always ready to forgive does not give us permission to live recklessly. Rather, it is a gift that calls us to be thankful that we have experienced God's love in and through human love and that when our human frailty causes us to fail, God's love can restore us to unity again.

QUESTIONS FOR COUPLES
TO DISCUSS

∞ Marriage Preparation

- Do you think you have a greater need for closeness or a greater need for distance? What about your partner?

- Identify other relationships that support each of you in times of trouble. Who are these people? When did the relationship begin? How often do you talk? When and where do you talk? What do you talk about?

- How comfortable are you with your partner's other relationships?

- How do you think you will respond to your partner's concerns about a relationship you have with someone else? What will you do or say?

- Do you or your partner have ongoing relationships with past lovers or spouses? Do any of them live in the area where you will live? How do you/will you establish and maintain boundaries in those relationships?

- What, for each of you, constitutes an affair?

- How do you think you would react to your partner being emotionally or sexually involved with someone else? What would you look for as warning signs? What would you do if you saw some of those signs?

- What do you think would make you vulnerable to an affair? What signs would you look for in yourself? What would you do if you saw some of those signs?

- What does "forsaking all others" and "be faithful to him [her] as long as you both shall live" mean to you? Whom might you need to forsake? What might you need to do to be faithful? Are you willing and able to do that?

- What did you learn from this chapter? If these questions raised any concerns, what do you want to do about them?

ⅎ Marriage Enrichment

- Do you think you have a greater need for closeness or a greater need for distance? What about your spouse?

- Identify other relationships that support each of you in times of trouble. Who are these people? When did the relationship begin? How often do you talk? When and where do you talk? What do you talk about?

- How comfortable are you with your spouse's other relationships?

- How do you respond to your spouse's concerns about a relationship you have with someone else? What do you do or say?

- Do you or your spouse have ongoing relationships with past lovers or spouses? Do any of them live in the area where you live? How have you established and maintained boundaries in those relationships? Do either of you feel any discomfort about the way those relationships are being handled?

- What, for each of you, constitutes an affair?

- How do you think you would react to your spouse being emotionally or sexually involved with someone else? What would you look for as warning signs? What would you do if you saw some of those signs?

- What do you think would make you vulnerable to an affair? What signs would you look for in yourself? What would you do if you saw some of those signs?

- What does "forsaking all others" and "be faithful to him [her] as long as you both shall live" mean to you? Did you need to forsake anyone when you got married? Whom might you need to forsake now? What did you need to do to remain faithful? What might you need to do now to remain faithful?

- What did you learn from this chapter? If these questions raised any concerns, what do you want to do about them?

QUESTIONS FOR GROUPS
TO DISCUSS

- How often do you/will you entertain or have guests in your home? Whom do you usually invite? Why might entertaining others become a problem in a marriage? What can it contribute to the marriage?

- Do you go out with others without your partner or have others in your home without your partner present? If not, why not? If so, under what conditions? How might different people react to this and why? How can a couple handle their different expectations?

- Do you have close friends? How have those relationships changed since your marriage, or how do you anticipate they will change after you marry? How have those relationships affected your relationship with your partner?

- Why do you think someone gets into an affair? How do you think affairs "happen"? What warning signs would you look for? What would you do?

- What does "forsaking all others" and "be faithful to him [her] as long as you both shall live" mean to you? Whom might a married person need to forsake? What might someone need to do to be faithful?

- Describe any relationship where you have seen trust broken. What actions broke that trust? What were the consequences? What could have prevented it? What did or could have healed it?

- Look at the quotation from the *Book of Common Prayer* at the beginning of this chapter. How has this prayer been a reality in your lives? What can/will you do to help it become more of a reality?

- If a couple wanted to seek marital or premarital counseling in your community, where could they go for help? Do you know someone you would recommend? For what types of concerns might it be better to see a clergyperson than a counselor? When might it be better to see a counselor than a clergyperson? When might it be best to talk with both? What are some of the differences between the help and support they offer?

- What did you learn from this chapter and discussion? Is there anything you plan to do because of what you learned?

SUGGESTED PROJECTS

- Keep a record, for a week or two, of the marriages shown in the television programs you watch or the stories you read in the paper, in books, or in magazines. What image of marriage does the media portray? How does it portray sexual relationships? Affairs? How might these images affect you and your marriage?

- Using the family tree you prepared after the last chapter, label each marriage in your family trees as strong, shaky, divorced, and so on. Interview your parents and other relatives to get a clearer sense of the well-being of the marital relationships in your families. Do any patterns emerge? What can you learn from those patterns? Does your relationship seem to fit any pattern?

FOUR

Living Together

Give them wisdom and devotion in the ordering of their common life.
(BCP 429)

In decades past, perhaps in your childhood, the family roles within many American homes were fairly standard: the father earned the money, took out the trash, mowed the lawn, and washed the car; the mother cooked, cleaned, shopped, and chauffeured the children; the children did a few "chores" for which they received an allowance. Today, the roles developed in families are rarely so neatly defined: each couple explores how they will accomplish the routine tasks of daily living and how they will build a shared life and home.

One of the major changes that has occurred is that most women now work outside the home for some or all of their adult lives. This reduces the time available for them to do housework and childcare by many hours each week. While the income from two wage earners is often necessary and the rewards of working are welcome, dual careers also increase the complexity of married life, which now must attend to the job demands and careers of two people while also managing the necessary duties of home and children.

It is helpful to discuss your role expectations before you marry so that you do not enter the relationship with widely different expectations. If you are already married, check to see how your expectations may have changed since your wedding. Be aware that even if you may *intellectually* expect that your lifestyle will be "liberated," your *emotional* expectations (perhaps hidden even from yourself) may be quite different. You may find that the expectations that emerge once you are married and "settled in" may be quite different from those with which you entered the marriage. Moreover, changing circumstances may change your roles. The discussion about roles needs to be repeated periodically.

Talk about how you make (or will make) work priority and career decisions. How do you support each other? How do you handle work-induced stress? Since many people still assume that the man's career matters but a woman merely does a job, it is important that you clarify the relative importance you place on each career and communicate that to others at work and in your personal lives. Your clarity will help others to support you.

Women who work full-time outside the home often continue to carry far more than half of the responsibilities related to home and childcare. Failure to address this imbalance in your relationship may lead to the woman being exhausted, hampered in her career development, and resentful. Inadequate time to build personal relationships and develop social interests can also lead to dissatisfaction. Men face new challenges as well. Many were raised in homes where their fathers had regular work, often at one company, with increasing salaries and responsibilities throughout life. Their mothers, if they worked, generally earned significantly less than their fathers. Today the woman may earn more than the man, often causing men considerable discomfort. In addition, both men and women can expect multiple job changes, stagnation, and even unemployment during their careers. Men who were raised to expect continuing career progression are often unprepared for this and thus may find themselves angry or depressed.

> ### *Chronic Health Problems*
>
> Does your partner have a chronic health problem or a family history of a health problem? If so, how do you handle it? How does your partner respond? Learn as much as you can about the problem. Visit with the partner's doctor. Read any information you can obtain. Talk with others who have the same problem. If special care is involved, learn how to do it, even if you will not be the care provider. It will help you understand what your partner faces and may be useful in an emergency situation where you may be called upon to provide the care.

Children add another level of complexity to this picture. Will one partner stay at home to care for young children? If not, who will care for them? Who will take off from work to stay with them when they are ill or need to go to the dentist? How will you balance work, personal needs and the needs of your children?

➡ Living with the Small Things

Besides these larger issues, there are a host of minor decisions that will affect your relationship. Common among these are:

- Social life: How often do you want to go out? To do what? With whom? Do you both enjoy the same events, go to what your partner likes, or each go your own way? How much do you spend? How much social time do you spend at job-related events?

- Appearance: What dress habits or lack of dress habits offend you? Do you expect him to shave every day? How do you react to her personal care rituals and hair curlers? Can each of you buy whatever clothes you want without consulting each other?

- Privacy: How much time does each of you need alone? Are you comfortable having each other listen in on phone calls? How do you feel about bathroom privacy? Are you comfortable with others coming into your bedroom or using your bathroom? Would you share a toothbrush, razor, or soap?

- Daily rhythms and habits: Are you a morning person or an evening person? Do you like silence or radio/TV/music when awake? When and where do you eat, exercise, engage in leisure activities? Do you expect to be alone or together while doing them? What constitutes "early" or "late" for each of you? How much preparation time do you need before you leave or before guests arrive?

- Cars, pets, and houses: Who drives the car? What are your driving and travel habits? Who cares for the car? Do you love or hate pets? Who takes care of them? What are your standards of neatness and cleanliness? What indoor temperature do you prefer? What style of decorating?

Each of these areas is a potential source of conflict in setting up and maintaining a common life. If you are unable to work out ways to adapt to each other's habits and needs, that conflict can slowly weaken your marriage. Both talking about these areas before the wedding and being willing to find compromises in your marriage are crucial to working out a comfortable pattern of life together.

Most couples fall into a division of labor based on their family experience or on societal expectations. When personal expectations are different, problems often occur. One way a couple can negotiate how they will divide up responsibilities is by doing the following exercise.

Deciding "Who Does What"

- Working separately, list every task you can identify. Include daily living, home and car maintenance, child care. Remember to include those things that only occur occasionally (taxes, cleaning closets, washing windows).

- Combine your individual lists and label each task as daily (D), weekly (W), monthly (M), and occasionally (O). (You may notice differences in your expectations as you assign these labels!) Make a copy of this master list so each of you has one.

- Working separately, label each item in the four groups as to whether you enjoy doing it (+), hate doing it (–) or are neutral about doing it (=). Be honest, but try to have roughly the same number in each category. No fair labeling them all (–)!

- Now compare lists. Any items that one partner has labeled (+) that the other partner has labeled (–) or (=) goes to the (+) partner. If both partners label an item (+), mark that item and hold it aside for the moment. If one person has an item marked (–) and the other has that item marked (=), give that item to the partner who feels neutral about it.

- Now take turns choosing one item at a time from the remaining (=) and (–) items. Each person now knows their partner's likes and dislikes and can take that into consideration.

- Finally, take turns choosing one item at a time from the ones you both like (+). You may want to "trade" one of these (+) items for two (=) or (–) items that may have been leftover at the end (assuming an odd number of items).

- When you're finished, review the whole list. Are both of you comfortable with it? If not, say why not and say what would make it work for you. Negotiate any changes. Then try it for awhile. Set a time when you will review it. If one person is uncomfortable with the task allocations, renegotiate the list.

Different "Standards of Care"

What do you do when one person has different standards for what is clean or how something is to be done? In our case Del is scrupulously neat and Linda is anything but tidy! Usually the person with a low tolerance for dirt or disorder or with high expectations for perfection ends up doing more of the work, spends lots of time trying to get the partner with lower standards to do things "my way," and/or ends up angry and frustrated.

The reality is that you can't change other people, you can only change yourself. You can negotiate and hope your partner changes his or her behavior, but each of you decides how much work you do and how you do it. Higher standards may motivate you to do more than your partner. If that bothers you, you can:

- decide that maintaining your standards is important, choose to do the extra work, and live with that choice;
- decide to lower your standards; or,
- decide to suspend your standards systematically over time, thus encouraging your partner to pick up the work you have left.

If you choose the last option, identify one or two items at a time and just ignore them. Eventually, your partner is likely to notice and comment that the trash bin is full. "Yes," you can respond, "it *is* full and it would be good to empty it." If your partner doesn't do it, leave it. If all else fails, suggest that "I'm going to do X; would you do Y? After we're finished we can work on Z together."

One important rule is that if you want help you need to accept it on the basis it is offered—that is, don't criticize how your partner does it or you will end up doing it alone again. While at times there may be a "right way" and a "wrong way" of doing something, in most cases there is simply a "different way." Consider each situation and ask yourself if it is worth the effort you are putting into it.

What happened to us? Linda has become a bit neater and bought a rolltop desk that can hide her papers. Del is more relaxed and tolerant about housekeeping chores. We each have specific chores, but we also share many tasks; Del does most of the cleaning, while Linda does all of the cooking and household shopping. This draws on both of our strengths and preferences and compensates for both of our weaknesses and dislikes.

❧ Thinking about the Future

While the immediate concerns of establishing a life together will predominate the discussion of those preparing for marriage, you need to think long-term as well. Those who have been married for some time may have already started this discussion; if not, now is a good time to do so!

As you think about your life together in the years to come, what are your hopes and dreams for the future? What do you value in life? What do you want to accomplish? If one partner wants to acquire a large home, a luxury car, and collect priceless artwork while the other wants to live simply, raise several children, and give generously to social causes, it may be difficult to build a common life together. Most couples will have somewhat similar goals, but they often do not plan how to achieve them. Identifying your long-term goals and discussing concrete actions can help you reach those goals.

Wills, Living Wills, and Organ Donation

The months before a wedding are not a time when one wants to think of death, but they are a good time to "get your affairs in order." Each partner should prepare a will shortly after the wedding. Dying without a will creates enormous problems and additional expense for your spouse. You may also want to discuss how to register bank accounts, cars, deeds, and other important documents with your lawyer in order to make it easy to settle your estate.

While you are focused on this area, it is useful to discuss your desires regarding life support, organ donation, and funeral arrangements. A Living Will (which specifies your desires for health care should you be unable to make decisions) is often prepared at the same time as a will that distributes property. You may also want discuss a power of attorney with your lawyer. This document allows the person you designate to make a variety of financial and legal decisions on your behalf should you become incapable of doing so yourself.

Finally, one of the most predictable realities is that you can't predict what the future will be like. The past twenty-five years have brought profound changes to homelife. The next twenty-five are likely to bring even more. What is important is that you review "who does what," common goals, and shared expectations regularly so you can adapt to changes in your life and in the world around you.

&c Making Your Home a Haven

Beyond the practical realities of learning how to "order your common life," most of us desire to make our homes a haven, a safe refuge from all the blows that may assault us. Another word for a safe haven is "sanctuary"—the same word we use for the sacred space in God's house. Christians seek to make their homes even more than a refuge. We seek to make our homes a sacred place where it is safe for us to be who we are, where we can rest and recover, be restored, renewed, and given a new lease on life.

In the marriage service we ask God to "bless them in their work and in their companionship; in their sleeping and in their waking; in their joys and in their sorrows" (BCP 430; BAS 534). We seek that blessing so that "their home may be a haven of blessing and peace" (BCP 431; BAS 534). That blessing and peace are meant for you, your family, and your friends. They are also meant for your neighbors, those who work for and with you, and for the stranger in the street.

The discussion about how we will live together goes far beyond just "who does what" or how we will balance work, children, and housework. How we live together as Christians proclaims the gospel more clearly to our neighbors and especially to our children than anything we can say. We can choose to live together in a way that creates a house, a place to live—or we can choose to live together in a way that creates a sanctuary, a sacred space.

Creating sacred space requires love and sacrifice. It means loving one another as Christ has loved us. And it often means "doing for" and "giving to" each other, not because you like to do that particular thing, but out of love. When two people marry, they cease being two separate people; they become a couple. Their life, from that day forward, is a life of "we" and not just "me." Thinking about the well-being of another person and choosing to contribute to that person's well-being, even at some cost to oneself, is a mark of maturity as a person and as a Christian. When we love, honor, and cherish each other, our home becomes a haven of blessing and peace to us and to all who come into that sacred space.

QUESTIONS FOR COUPLES
TO DISCUSS

ঔ Marriage Preparation

- Negotiate a division of labor: Who will shop for food? Who will buy other supplies? Who will cook, clean, do yard work, keep the car running? If you are already living together, do the "who will do what?" exercise in this chapter and then compare the results to what you actually do now. Reflect on how you conducted the negotiation. Plan when you will review and renegotiate.

- Do you consider yourself a slob or a "neatnik" or somewhere in-between? How do you think your standards for how things should be done might affect your life together? What will each of you do to minimize the negative effects?

- What do you expect (or know) will be a problem in living together? Review the "large issues" and the list of smaller annoyances this chapter discusses. Identify three or four things you might do to overcome each of those problems. Agree on one solution to try and a second solution to try if your first choice doesn't work out.

- If both of you work (or plan to work), what are your individual work/career goals? How will you decide whose career takes priority (especially when relocation is required)?

- What would you define as "excessive" or "inadequate" time or energy being put into work? Compare your individual answers and agree on a definition. How will you recognize and deal with "workaholism" in one or both partners? What impact do you think it might have on your marriage? How will you deal with "inadequate" time or energy devoted to work? What impact do you think it might have on your marriage?

- How will you handle unemployment by one and by both of you? What preparation will you make for it? What will you do while you are unemployed? How will you support your partner during his or her unemployment?

- Where would you like to live in five years? ten years? In what kind of home? city? environment? What do you imagine you and your partner doing? What three things will be most important to you? Compare your individual answers.

- What will you do to make your home a sacred space?

- What did you learn from this chapter? Is there anything you plan to do because of what you have learned?

༄ Marriage Enrichment

- What problems in living together have you experienced? Review the large issues and the smaller annoyances discussed in the chapter. Identify three or four things you might do to overcome each of those problems. Agree on one solution to try and a second solution to try if your first choice doesn't work out.

- What is the division of labor in your home? Are you satisfied with it? Do the exercise on how to negotiate a division of labor in this chapter and then compare the results to the way you do things now. Reflect on how you conducted the negotiation. If one or both of you want to try a different arrangement, agree to try it for awhile. Plan when you will review and renegotiate.

- Do you consider yourself a slob or a "neatnik" or somewhere in-between? How have your standards for how things should be done affected your life together? What has each of you done and/or will each of you do to minimize the negative effects?

- If both of you work (or plan to work in the future), what are your individual work/career goals? How have you/will you decide whose career takes priority (especially when relocation is required)?

- What would you define as "excessive" or "inadequate" time or energy being put into work? Compare your individual answers and agree on a definition. How will you recognize and deal with "workaholism" in one or both spouses? What impact do you think it has or might have on your marriage? How do you or will you deal with "inadequate" time or energy devoted to work? What impact does it have or do you think it might have on your marriage?

- How will you handle unemployment of one or both of you? What preparation will you make for it? What will you do while you are unemployed? How will you support your spouse during his or her unemployment? If unemployment has already occurred, discuss how you handled it or are handling it and what changes you might make in your behavior next time.

- Where would you like to live in five years? ten years? In what kind of home? city? environment? What do you imagine you and your spouse doing? What three things will be most important things to you? Compare your answers.

- What are you doing to make your home a sacred space?

- What did you learn from this chapter? Is there anything you plan to do because of what you have learned?

> ## QUESTIONS FOR GROUPS
> ## TO DISCUSS

- When you were a child, what were the roles in your family? Do you want to repeat those or do something different?

- Do either/both of you work? In what jobs? Do you anticipate job/career changes? What other jobs might either of you hold in the future?

- How do you understand the relationship between work and home, your job and your marriage/family? Discuss "workaholism," unemployment, career conflicts, and other stresses created by your work.

- How do you divide up home responsibilities? How do you feel about your division of labor? Does it match what each of you wants or needs? If you recently negotiated a new agreement, how did you feel about the negotiations?

- Discuss the "large issues" and the smaller annoyances identified in this chapter. Which of them do you think could become real problems in a marriage? How? What might a couple do to address these problems? What problems in living together have you encountered? What impact do you think those problems have on your marriage? What ideas do you have for how couples might address some of those problems?

- Review and discuss the three prayers quoted in this chapter:

  Give them wisdom and devotion in the ordering of their common life, that each may be to the other a strength in need, a counselor in perplexity, a comfort in sorrow, and a companion in joy. (BCP 429)

  Let their love for each other be a seal upon their hearts, a mantle about their shoulders, and a crown upon their foreheads. Bless them in their work and in their companionship; in their sleeping and in their waking; in their joys and in their sorrows; in their life and in their death. (BCP 430)

Send therefore your blessing upon these your servants, that they may so love, honor and cherish each other in faithfulness and patience, in wisdom and true godliness, that their home may be a haven of blessing and peace. (BCP 431)

- What is your understanding of making your home a sanctuary, of creating sacred space? How do you do that now? How do you want to do that in the future?

- What did you learn from this chapter? Is there anything you plan to do because of what you learned that you would like to share with others in the group?

SUGGESTED PROJECTS

- Using the family tree you prepared at the end of the last chapter, mark any individuals whom you know or strongly suspect to have been alcoholics, drug addicts, or substance abusers. Can you identify patterns? If you see the same behavior in two or more generations and/or in two or more persons in your family blood line, discuss the implications of this with a counselor trained in addiction and abuse therapy. The more family members with a history of addiction or abuse, the more likely it is that you will suffer from the same affliction. Early intervention and preventive action can save you untold grief. It is better to be too cautious in this matter than to ignore the signs of trouble. Often your life and/or the life of your partner or children is at risk.

- Interview a couple about the relationship between home and work and how they dealt with the issues in their situation. (This might occur as part of a married couples' group session.)

- Interview a couple you know who have made their home a sanctuary. Find out what they did to create and maintain that sacred space.

Fighting Fair

Give them grace, when they hurt each other, to recognize and acknowledge
their fault, and to seek each other's forgiveness and yours.
(BCP 429)

Having fights with your partner is not unusual, nor is it "bad." In fact, couples who do not fight at all are often more at risk for marital failure. People who live in an intimate relationship with each other for any significant length of time will have disagreements. The problems come in how those disagreements are handled. The trick is to learn how to fight fairly.

ॐ Unfair Fights

Some people fight physically, some are verbally abusive, and still others fight by refusing to fight. All these techniques are destructive and dangerous. The fact that physical fights are not fair (or right) is easy to understand. No one should ever physically injure another person. This includes slapping, pinching, kicking, or hitting. It does not matter if the injury is mild or substantial, or whether it was done "in fun." A rule of thumb is that if the other person protests, even mildly, or if either of you has the slightest doubt about whether something is "right" or not, don't do it. Physical abuse is wrong and, in most cases, it is illegal. If you are in a relationship that includes physical abuse, seek professional help immediately.

Verbal fights can also be destructive. Obviously, calling someone names or insulting them is abusive. However, teasing them about a shortcoming, making fun of them, or constantly nagging them about a failure can also be abusive. Ask yourself: "Would someone who truly loved me do this to me?" or "Would I want my child to be treated this way?" If you don't want the behavior for yourself or your child, don't do it. Some destructive verbal fight techniques are less obvious. When you live with and love someone, you come to know things about your partner that other people don't know. Often this is information about his or her vulnerabilities, embarrassing or painful stories you were told, or experiences you have observed. It is unfair to use this information against your partner in a fight (often called "hitting below the belt").

Several kinds of verbal fights, though not necessarily abusive, certainly are not helpful. The "kitchen sink fight" starts with one topic and then gets every problem from the last couple of years dumped into it. Likewise, in a "gunny sack fight" the anger and annoyance from a long series of upsets is stored up until some minor incident triggers an outburst completely out of proportion to the situation. The "sniper fight" is when one person's anger comes out in a series of snipes (not-so-funny jokes, digs, and snide remarks). When the other person protests or asks what is wrong, the sniper innocently claims that "nothing" is generating the behavior or even that the partner is imagining things or exaggerating. The "kick-the-dog fight" is when anger from somewhere outside the relationship (often work) is projected into the marriage and the other partner gets "kicked" merely because he or she is there. These and other verbal fights that hurt or demean your partner are destructive to your partner, to the relationship, and to your self-worth.

Finally, there are people who fight by refusing to fight. One type refuses to fight by becoming weak and highly oversensitive to pain. Any hint of disagreement sends them into agony and tears. Their partners feel helpless and often feel "at fault" for even bringing up the subject and "causing" the hurt. Meanwhile, the wounded partner avoids dealing with any conflict and the disagreements remain unresolved. Other fight-refusers become silent and withdrawn but, when asked, claim "nothing" is bothering them and "nothing" is wrong. They may even become very nice and especially polite. In either

---

Be Angry, But Do Not Sin

There's nothing wrong with being angry; it's a normal human emotion. The problems usually occur when our anger pushes us to act in ways that hurt or we nurse our anger for days. The advice given in Ephesians is simple, direct, and effective:

Be angry, but do not sin; do not let the sun go down on your anger and do not make room for the devil. Put away from you all bitterness and wrath and wrangling and slander, together with all malice, and be kind to one another, tenderhearted, forgiving one another, as God in Christ has forgiven you....Be imitators of God and live in love.

(Eph. 4:26-27, 31–5:2)

case, they are angry and have some unresolved issue but they choose to conduct an unfair fight by refusing to fight. This "freezes" the intimacy of the relationship by effectively cutting off dialogue. This fighter's partner is left powerless, not knowing what the problem is or how to address it. The mixed message (distancing, which conveys anger, while innocently claiming nothing is wrong) often makes this fighter's partner feel crazy, not able to trust his or her own instincts.

Communicating openly and honestly is the key to good fighting. Unfair fight techniques destroy good communication. A "ragaholic" gets charged up and rants and raves with no space for any dialogue. An abuser hits, physically or verbally, to shut off communication. A "poor-me" victim gets sad-eyed or weepy and derails dialogue by claiming to be hurt and unable to bear anything. Those who refuse to fight silence dialogue with their silence.

⅋ Understanding Abuse

No one has the right to physically hurt others, force them to have sexual encounters against their will, or emotionally abuse them (by degrading them, calling them names, insulting or shaming them, making fun of them). Not your spouse. Not your parent. Not an authority figure. No one.

Abusers will often try to make you feel that something you have said or done "caused" them to abuse you or that the abuse is legitimate punishment. This is an excuse. There is no reason for one person to abuse another.

Abusers will often become very repentant and even tearful; they will promise not to repeat the behavior and will plead with you to forgive them. They may be sincere, but someone who abuses once will usually abuse again. In fact, abuse usually gets progressively worse. Forgiving an abuser again and again merely makes you an enabler—someone who enables another person to continue abusive or destructive behaviors by denying, ignoring, or covering up that behavior.

If you see some of the following signs in your partner you may be in a relationship with someone who will become seriously abusive:

- Falls madly in love with you and pushes for exclusive commitment almost immediately.
- Is excessively possessive and jealous; constantly checks up on you.
- Begins to isolate you from family and friends; wants you to quit working or going out with others.
- Is controlling; keeps all the money; makes you ask for permission to go out; demands an accounting of where you go, who you talk to, what you say, what you spent.

- Expects perfection from you and others; expects that his or her every need will be met.
- Blames others for all problems, mistakes; sees others at fault for normal things in life that don't happen to meet his or her standards or desires.
- Makes others responsible for his or her feelings: "You make me mad" or "You make me happy" instead of "I feel mad when...."
- Is cruel to animals: kicks the dog, tells stories of killing a cat or bird.
- Is cruel to children: teases them until they cry; hits them; expects them to do things far beyond their capability and punishes them when they fail.
- Is destructive of property: throws things; breaks things (especially things you value).
- Talks about previous situations in which he or she hit a partner but has an excuse for this behavior.
- Enjoys rough sex; tickles or holds you down despite your protests; finds the idea of rape exciting; pushes you to do things you do not want to do.
- Is verbally abusive: calls you names; makes fun of you; constantly criticizes.
- Flips suddenly from being "super nice" to being extremely angry.
- Threatens to "break your neck" or "kill you"; sees this as normal behavior.

If you see several of these signs in your relationship, it is time to get help or get out. If you are preparing for marriage but are already experiencing abuse, we urge you to defer marriage plans and seek professional help. If you are already married or are living together, seek professional help promptly. You may need to live separately while you resolve the abuse issue or decide to end the relationship. Since the abuser usually has no motivation to change, the person being abused generally must act first.

Dealing with Abuse

At the *first* instance of abuse, tell the abuser that you will not accept such behavior and that together you will seek professional help now. If he or she refuses, go yourself. In consultation with a professional, you *may* choose to give the person *one* more chance.

At the *second* instance of abuse, leave immediately for a safer environment. Abusers will continue to abuse unless you say "no." Each instance makes it harder.

DO NOT ACCEPT ABUSE. There are many groups and professionals that can help you. Reach out. Do not wait. Do not stay with an abuser, and do not accept abuse.

If either or both of you have experienced significant abuse as a child, seek professional help. It is *highly likely* that this abuse will have a negative impact on your marriage and/or family life unless it is addressed promptly. It may be necessary to seek help at several key points during the marriage, as pivotal changes in the family's life (the birth of a child or loss of a job, for example) can trigger feelings and behaviors.

If the abuse from outside your relationship is still current, it is essential that the person who was abused be protected from the abuser. This is necessary even if it means cutting off a relationship with a family member. It is also important to protect those whom an abuser might abuse in the future. For example, an uncle who sexually molested you as a child should never be allowed alone with your children—even if he is now "an old man." The danger that he will repeat his abusive behavior is too high to risk a child's well-being.

❧ Rights and Responsibilities

Rights help us understand what we are entitled to expect and receive as human beings. Responsibilities help us understand what is expected of us. Rights and responsibilities are two sides of the same coin. The goal is to balance rights with responsibilities and vice versa. The following list of responsibilities could be reworded as a list of basic human rights. In a marriage, we have a responsibility to:

- Listen to our partner and respond politely.
- Respect our partner's opinions, even if we disagree with them.
- Hear and acknowledge our partner's feelings as real.
- Respect our partner's work, projects, interests, and organizations.
- Address our partner by a name he or she prefers.
- Refrain from abusing or threatening our partner, either physically or emotionally.
- Refrain from blaming, judging, or criticizing our partner for who he or she is or what he or she does.
- Request what we want or need, rather than order.
- Give good will, encouragement, and emotional support to our partner.
- Support our partner as he or she seeks to be happy, fulfilled, and loved.

Beyond these basic human rights and responsibilities, the marriage service in the *Book of Common Prayer* calls us as Christians to:

- Love, honor, and cherish our partner until the day we die.
- Be faithful to him or her, forsaking all others.

- Give all that we have and all that we are to our partner; give even our will so our wills may be knit together in God's will.
- Be a strength in need, a counselor in perplexity, a comfort in sorrow, and a companion in joy.
- Recognize and acknowledge our faults and seek our partner's and God's forgiveness.
- Become a sign of Christ's love to this sinful and broken world.
- Bring up our children to know, love, and serve God.
- Reach out in love and concern for others.

Good Fights

Good fights are dialogues—sometimes heated!—in which disagreements are honestly expressed by both individuals who are working to understand each other's viewpoint and seeking to negotiate a mutually acceptable solution. These disagreements strengthen the relationship rather than undermine, weaken, or destroy it.

Good fights require good communication. Some primary skills in good communication include:

- *Listen to what is really being said*—look for verbal and nonverbal cues, feelings as well as information; try to understand better what the other is saying rather than gathering ammunition for your response.
- *Speak for yourself*—"I feel," "I want/need" rather than "You are," "Everyone knows that you...."
- *Avoid should's and ought's*—"You should have" or "I ought to."
- *Ask for what you want*—be as open and honest as you can about what you really feel, what you want, what you need.
- *Understand and accept differences*—between men and women, between different personalities, between you and your partner.
- *Focus on what was done (or not done)*—not on the person, his or her faults and character defects.
- *Affirm each other regularly*—it makes hearing any bad news much easier!

Most marriages falter because of a lack of good communication rather than outright abuse or incompatibility. It is worth the time and effort needed to learn to communicate with clarity and love. Commitment and practice are needed, along with the desire to experiment and see what works best for you.

There are several communication tactics you may want to try. If emotions are high, it may be helpful to have a fight at a time other than the moment when a disagreement occurs. You can **agree** to discuss the matter when both of you have calmed down and can give the matter your undivided attention. This is especially true if you have children and need to find times when they are in bed or otherwise occupied and thus unlikely to interrupt you. Fighting in front of children often leads them to intervene in ways that disrupt your communication and may put them in the middle.

In the early days of our relationship we discovered that late night phone calls were a very effective way for us to discuss significant and/or painful topics. (In fact, we still call each other to settle an argument from a separate line on the other side of the house!) The telephone can be a very intimate, focused means of communication while still providing enough distance to make it "safe" to talk about "hot" issues.

Complaint, Criticism, or Contempt

- A complaint is *specific*, limited to one situation. It states how you feel. ("I am upset because you didn't take out the garbage tonight.")

- A criticism tends to be global and includes blaming your partner. You'll often find the word "always" or "never" in a criticism. ("You never take out the garbage. Now it's overflowed and that's your fault. I can't ever rely on you.")

- Contempt adds insult to the criticism. It is verbal character assassination in which you accuse your spouse of stupidity, incompetence, etc. ("You idiot, why can't you ever remember to take out the garbage?")

The goal is to state your complaint. To prevent yourself from slipping into criticism or contempt, observe the following general guidelines:

- Remove the blame from your comments.

- Say how *you* feel.

- Don't criticize your partner's personality.

- Don't insult, mock, or use sarcasm.

- Be direct.

- Stick with one situation.

- Don't try to analyze your partner's personality.

- Don't mind-read.

(from *Why Marriages Succeed or Fail* by John Gottman)

Phone calls or written notes are distancing methods that can help calm emotions and foster more honest communication between partners who may not be as comfortable in a face-to-face encounter. Some couples find it helpful to discuss problems at a specific time, perhaps doing a weekly "check-in" to resolve any issues that may have come up during the week. Other couples plan to address issues as promptly as possible. Each couple needs to work out a system of working through disagreements that fits who they are and is effective for them. There are a host of self-help books that will enable you to learn more about fair and unfair ways of fighting.

⇛ Understanding Differences

People respond to disagreements quite differently depending on their personality, life experience, culture, and gender. It is important to understand and appreciate these differences as you develop your way of working out disagreements. For example, some people work out problems by talking about them immediately; others like to mull them over first and then talk. Some people are bothered by many things; others are rarely bothered by anything. Some people get very angry (hot anger) but get over it quickly; others push anger below the surface (cold anger) and freeze others out. Both need to work at getting their anger into the "warm anger" range where it can be expressed and handled safely. Good communication skills often enable you to prevent an annoyance from becoming anger in the first place.

It is helpful to explore your differ-

Communication Differences

Current research indicates that men and women communicate differently. Men tend to solve problems, while women use conversation to express feelings, work through ideas, and build rapport. Neither style of communication is wrong, but it can be extremely frustrating if the two of you are in different modes and don't realize it.

If you don't seem to be communicating, try labelling your conversation as "feelings-oriented" or "problem-solving" in order to recognize the validity and importance of both communication styles while choosing to use one or the other at that point in time. (See *Now That I'm Married, Why Isn't Everything Perfect?* by Susan Page)

ences in personality and how that affects the way you approach disagreements. Look also at the cultural influences that may affect how you handle disagreements. Different cultures encourage different responses to conflict. Our perceptions and the suggestions we have given here are based on our cultural norms. Those raised in

---

Bearing All Things

Love is patient; love is kind; love is not envious or boastful or arrogant or rude. It does not insist on its own way; it is not irritable or resentful; it does not rejoice in wrongdoing, but rejoices in the truth. It bears all things, believes all things, hopes all things, endures all things.

(1 Cor. 13:4-7)

What does this passage tell us about handling disagreements within a Christian marriage? When might "bearing or enduring all things" create problems? What are we called to bear or endure in each other?

---

and/or living in other cultures may have other ways of handling disagreements, and we encourage you to discuss them with each other and your family members. This becomes especially important if the two of you are from different cultural backgrounds.

It is also important that you understand how anger and disagreements were handled in your childhood. Often people either absorb their parents' or caregiver's approach, or they react to it by doing the opposite. Significant experiences can also shape how one reacts to disagreements or anger. For example, someone who has experienced serious injury in a disagreement may be overly fearful or overly aggressive in response to disagreements later in life. Telling these stories can help you understand yourselves and each other and thus find ways to counteract previous experiences or personality traits that contribute to unfair or unproductive fighting.

∞ Understanding Stress and Transitions

Disagreements tend to escalate in times of stress or transition. While this does not excuse abusive behavior or unfair fighting techniques, it may help you anticipate times when you might be more prone to disagreements. Often the conflicts are less severe when you realize that there are contributory factors that may be beyond the precipitating event. The conflicts may even be avoided by acknowledging the stress and taking action to help you deal with it. A regular check on your stress level and your response to stress can help you anticipate problems and plan ways to deal with them. Significant changes that often generate more fights than normal include:

- *Changes in your home life*—getting married, separated, or divorced; having a child; experiencing greater difficulties or success at work or school than usual; illnesses; changes in one's extended family; moving or remodeling a house; anything that changes the content or quality of life in your home.

- *Changes in your work/school or finances*—a promotion; getting fired; changing jobs; retiring; getting a new boss; advancing in your career faster than expected or discovering that advancement is blocked; co-workers leaving or coming; corporate restructuring; an increase or decrease in salary; starting or stopping school; an inheritance, windfall, or lottery; assuming loans or paying off loans; large new bills or ongoing large bills paid off.

- *Personal or inner changes*—getting sick or recovering from an illness; changing your appearance, your eating or sleeping habits, or your sexual activities; getting into or out of an affair; experiencing any notable success or failure; experiencing changes in your lifestyle, self-image, or values; experiencing a spiritual awakening or a loss of faith; discovering a new dream or losing an old one.

Obviously all of us will experience some of these transitions during our lifetime. It is important to be aware that such life transitions increase stress and create opportunities for more than usual levels of conflict. Again, the point is not to avoid transitions or excuse inappropriate behaviors, but to heighten your awareness of when conflicts are more likely to occur so you can respond in a positive and healthy way. A little extra tender, loving care for yourself and your partner can help you get through the tough times.

&o Reconciliation

The common phrase "kiss and make up" reflects a very human desire to restore unity to a relationship we have with someone we love. Christians are called to go even beyond that human desire. Marriage is a sacrament because it shows outwardly the inward reality of unity: "Make their life

> ### Bearing Each Other's Burdens
>
> *Bear one another's burdens, and in this way you will fulfill the law of Christ.* (Gal. 6.2)
>
> Bearing each other's burdens means going beyond forgiveness. It means taking onto yourself the consequences of something your partner did. This kind of selfless love is what Christ showed on the cross. We "fulfill the law of Christ"—that is, we become like Christ—when we do that for each other. One of the joys of a marriage partnership is discovering that someone loves you enough to suffer the consequence for a wrong you did or to do whatever it takes to make it right again.

together a sign of Christ's love to this sinful and broken world, that unity may overcome estrangement, forgiveness heal guilt, and joy conquer despair" (BCP 429). In order for Christian couples to be that sign, they must live that reality.

We are called to love, honor, and cherish one another. That love and God's grace enables a couple to "recognize and acknowledge their fault, and to seek each other's forgiveness" (BCP 429). It is difficult to admit that we are wrong. Most of us want to justify what we did, explain it away, or declare that the impact it had was insignificant. But often our actions and words hurt others, whether we intend that hurt or not. The person who is hurt is the one who defines what actions or words are hurtful; the other person then must decide whether he or she wishes to create that pain again by repeating those actions or words.

Learning to say, "When you did/said XX I felt hurt/angry/betrayed" openly, honestly, and without attacking the other person is the first step. The other person needs to understand the impact of the words or actions before he or she can have a real choice to do anything different. Saying "I'm sorry. I will not do that again; I will do things differently" is the next step. When we hear the impact we had on our

---

The Process of Reconciliation

"All have sinned and fall short of the glory of God" (Romans 3:23). The church recognizes the sinfulness of all of us, the potential each of us has to break the relationship between ourselves and God, each other, and the creation—even to break apart from our own being. The basic elements of the service of *The Reconciliation of a Penitent* are helpful in any situation. *(The following notes are written with serious offenses in mind such as abuse, addiction, or affairs, but the steps apply for all levels of offenses.)*

CONFESS OUR SIN: Recognize and acknowledge honestly before God and other Christians what you have done; feel the guilt and sorrow that comes with seeing the pain you have caused; accept responsibility for your actions.

MAKE AMENDS: Do whatever you can to "make it right" for those affected by your action; apologize; pay for therapy or for pain and suffering; resign from a position of leadership; spend time in prison.

SEEK AMENDMENT OF LIFE: Do whatever is necessary to make sure that you do not repeat the behavior again; participate in therapy; join a self-help group; take medication; remove yourself from situations of temptation; change jobs; change your lifestyle.

ACCEPT FORGIVENESS: Receive forgiveness as a gift and rejoice in it; be healed; embrace wholeness; bear witness to God's love.

These four things provide the basic elements needed for reconciliation and wholeness.

— Excerpt from *A Covenant of Trust* by Linda L. Grenz
(Cincinnati: Forward Movement Publications)

partner, we can choose to change. Making amends is often necessary and usually helpful.

Saying "I forgive" is the last step. When we have said how the action/words affected us and heard our partner apologize and commit to change, then we can and need to forgive—to wipe that incident out of our "record books" and move on. Then we can experience reconciliation, being restored to unity with each other.

This may sound simple, and in some respects it is. Commitment to each other and consistent practice (and it does take practice) will enable you to build a strong, loving relationship with each other. It will also give you the courage to forgive, to seek reconciliation, and to exercise a ministry of reconciliation in other places—at work or in your community. Practicing the ministry of reconciliation at home teaches us to become more effective ministers of reconciliation elsewhere. And when that happens the marriage journey becomes an ongoing sacrament—an outward and visible sign of the inward and spiritual grace of being "restored to unity with God and one another in Christ" (BCP 855).

QUESTIONS FOR COUPLES TO DISCUSS

⁊ Marriage Preparation

- How did your parents or other adult caregivers fight? Was there any physical, emotional, or verbal abuse? What would you identify as the most destructive ways they fought? the healthiest ways? How did you feel when you heard them disagree or fight? What did you do?

- Describe how you and your parents or adult caregivers handled disagreements at different stages in life: when you were very young, when you were a teenager, when you were a young adult. How do you handle disagreements with them now?

- Has either of you ever been hit, slapped, had something thrown at you, been screamed at or called names? Describe the situation and discuss how you felt about it. Have you ever done any of these things to anyone else? If so, describe the situation, how you felt, what you did, and what you learned as a result.

- How do the two of you handle disagreements? What do the two of you fight about now? What do you think you will fight about after you're married? How do you fight? Do you fight in public? Do you hold grudges?

- Look at your responses to the questions above and at each of your personal histories. Identify patterns you can see and talk about what might happen in the future.

- How do you feel about your current way of handling disagreements? Are you satisfied with things as they are? If not, what changes do you want to make?

- When you are angry with someone else, what is the most helpful thing your partner can do? When you are angry with your partner, what is most helpful?

- Review the fair fighting/good communication skills listed in this chapter. Which do you feel you use consistently and effectively? Which would you like to practice and improve?

- Look at the prayer in the marriage service at the beginning of this chapter. Discuss how reconciliation occurs in your relationship. How do you think practicing the ministry of reconciliation at home can help you become better ministers of reconciliation in other aspects of your lives?

- What did you learn from this chapter? What decisions do you choose to make in response to what you learned?

৯ Marriage Enrichment

- How did your parents or other adult caregivers fight? Was there any physical, emotional, or verbal abuse? What would you identify as the most destructive ways they fought? the healthiest ways? How did you feel when you heard them disagree or fight? What did you do?

- Describe how you and your parents or adult caregivers handled disagreements at different stages in life: when you were very young, when you were a teenager, when you were a young adult. How do you handle disagreements with them now?

- Has either of you ever been hit, slapped, had something thrown at you, been screamed at or called names? Describe the situation and discuss how you felt about it. Have you ever done any of these things to anyone else? If so, describe the situation, how you felt, what you did, and what you learned as a result.

- How do the two of you handle disagreements? What do you fight about? How do you fight? Do you fight in public? Do you hold grudges?

- Look at your responses to the questions above and at each of your personal histories. Identify patterns you can see and talk about how they affect you now or how they might affect you in the future.

- If you have children, how do you handle disagreements with them? How do they handle disagreements with you, with each other, or with others? What have they learned from you? What do you want them to learn?

- How do you feel about your current way of handling disagreements? Are you satisfied with things as they are? If not, what changes do you want to make?

- When you are angry at someone else, what is the most helpful thing your spouse can do? When you are angry with your spouse, what is most helpful?

- Review the fair fighting/good communication skills listed in this chapter. Which do you feel you use consistently and effectively? Which would you like to practice and improve?

- Look at the prayer in the marriage service quoted at the beginning of this chapter. Discuss how reconciliation occurs in your marriage. How does practicing the ministry of reconciliation at home help you become better ministers of reconciliation in other aspects of your lives?

- What did you learn from this chapter? What decisions do you choose to make in response to what you learned?

QUESTIONS FOR GROUPS TO DISCUSS

- Talk about how your families handled disagreements when you were younger and how they handle them now.

- How do you fight? What do you fight about? How do you know when a fight has become destructive or abusive? What do you do when it does? Make a list of agencies or people you would consider going to for help if you needed it.

- How do you respond when your partner fights with someone else? If you have children, compare your reactions to seeing your partner fight with others and how the two of you handle conflicts with your children. Can you see any patterns? What are some strategies couples without children might adopt to better prepare them to handle conflicts with children later?

- When you are angry with someone else, what is the most helpful thing your partner can do? When you are angry with your partner, what is most helpful?

- Build a list of behaviors that might be considered abusive. Write each suggestion on newsprint or a blackboard. Then take a few minutes while each person considers whether he or she thinks the behavior is abusive and puts a Y (yes), N (no), or M (maybe) next to each suggestion. Discuss the two lists. See if you can agree on which items to include. Discuss any items over which you disagree.

- Build a list of "rights" you feel all humans have and use the same process to check for agreement. Discuss any items over which you disagree. Review the list under "Rights and Responsibilities" in this chapter. Are there any patterns in the way you see rights or abusive behaviors, such as age, gender, or past experiences?

- Discuss how you handled any disagreements that occurred in the group as you worked through the last two questions. What did you learn about yourself, each other, and ways of resolving disagreements?

- Review the fair fighting/good communication skills listed in this chapter. Which do you feel you use consistently and effectively? Which would you like to practice and improve? What other good communication strategies have you discovered?

- Look at the prayer in the marriage service from the beginning of this chapter. How does reconciliation occur in your relationship? How do you think practicing the ministry of reconciliation at home can help you become better ministers of reconciliation in other aspects of your lives?

- What did you learn from this chapter? What decisions do you choose to make in response to what you learned?

SUGGESTED PROJECTS

- Take notes on any disagreement you experience or observe this week (at work, at home, on the street, on television). How did those involved choose to handle their disagreement? How did you respond emotionally or in what you did or said? What did you learn?

- Take notes on disagreements the two of you have had recently. How did you handle those disagreements? Do you handle disagreements with each other differently than disagreements with other people? Can you identify any patterns? If so, imagine that pattern escalating and extending for ten or twenty years: how do you feel about living with this pattern of handling disagreements? Then imagine that pattern decreasing over time: what would cause your behaviors to change?

❧ SIX

Money Matters

...with all that I am, and all that I have, I honor you.
(BCP 427)

The old saying that "money is power" has a painful grain of truth in it. Because money is power, it can be a major source of conflict in a marital relationship. In some marriages, the wage earner uses that power by insisting that it is "my money" so "I decide how it gets spent." In some marriages couples hide assets, debts, or expenditures from each other. Some spouses don't even know how much the other earns, and many people who are planning to marry do not know how much their prospective mate owns or owes.

In the past, many marriages survived reasonably well with one spouse (usually the husband) making and controlling the money. The negative impact of this on the marital relationship was often not obvious to either partner—it was just the way things were done. The power imbalance was accepted or ignored, and its impact on the wife was often invisible until her husband died and suddenly she had to make financial decisions without any experience and with limited knowledge. Widowhood for many women made the negative effects of their imbalanced relationship painfully real.

Today it is generally acknowledged that full disclosure and communication about money matters contributes to a healthy marital relationship. This is especially true in Christian marriage, where we pledge our honor to one another "with all that I am, and all that I have." It's hard to pledge something we keep hidden. The first step a couple needs to take is to be completely honest with each other about what they own, what they owe, what they earn, and what they spend. Money *does* matter: how you handle your money can support your relationship—or undermine it.

ಬ The Value of Money

We all have very different attitudes about money and its place in our lives. Some people grew up in a home where a lack of money was not a concern; they may assume that the money they need will always be available. Others grew up in an environment where there was a great deal of concern about money; they may assume that money, even if available or abundant now, will disappear when they most need it. For some people *earning* lots of money is important; for others *spending* it is important, and for still others *having* money is important. And then there are people who don't care about earning or spending or having money at all!

Each of these different values about money affects your lifestyle and your relationship. Usually difficulties arise when one or both partners hold one of these values to an extreme, or when the two partners have widely differing values about money. One person may spend freely, while the other wants to hoard every penny. One person may be comfortable with large debts and high credit card balances, while the other may be anxious about any debt. Any value carried to an extreme can create financial difficulties and conflicts in a marriage.

Our values about money usually are influenced by our childhood and early adult experiences and by the

> ### *The Love of Money*
>
> *We brought nothing into the world, so that we can take nothing out of it; but if we have food and clothing, we will be content with these. But those who want to be rich fall into temptation and are trapped by many senseless and harmful desires that plunge people into ruin and destruction. For the love of money is the root of all kinds of evil, and in their eagerness to be rich some have wandered away from the faith and pierced themselves with many pains.* (1 Tim. 6:7-10)
>
> How can money create pain in your life? What can you do to make money a positive force in your life?

attitudes and values of our parents and other caregivers. Understanding your history is an important part of understanding how you respond to money. Take the time to look at your history and identify differences in how you were raised. Think about how you live now and any adjustments you will have to make to your lifestyle. Discuss practical realities and the feelings that result from them. In doing so, you can choose either to continue acting in ways you "picked up" from your childhood or to adopt new patterns of behavior. You can also find ways to handle feelings you may have if significant lifestyle adjustments are required.

The goal is to work toward a balance in your marriage and thus use money wisely. You may achieve that balance naturally because both of you are basically in the middle of the spectrum of values and behaviors relating to money. Or you may achieve that balance because one of you is a spender, the other a hoarder, and the two of you understand, acknowledge, and affirm the role each of you plays in keeping your joint money management balanced. In either case, the result is that your relationship is sustained rather than undermined by the role money plays in it.

&   Earning Money

Most people feel good about earning money. In our society we tend to measure our self-worth by the jobs we have and how much we earn. This works well if you earn a reasonable amount of money. It works even better if you earn more than you expected to earn. It does not work well if you earn less than you expected or, even worse, are unemployed and/or unable to earn an income. Even families that choose to have only one wage earner often find that the partner who works without a salary feels "worth-less" because of the subtle messages society sends about money and worth.

Discuss how you feel about your income and how much you want to earn in the future. Decide as a couple what it important to you and set your goals accordingly. Develop a backup plan for what you will do if the unexpected happens (layoffs or new opportunities). If any of these plans are counter to the prevailing culture or either family's values, be aware that you will need to discuss your feelings regularly. Consciously affirm yourselves for doing what you choose to do rather than what the culture or your family history dictates. Often you can prevent low self-esteem by being clear about your choices and the reasons for it, especially if and when you are challenged by family, friends, or colleagues. Being able to say, clearly and calmly, "We understand that you have different values about money, but this is the choice we have made" can derail potential conflicts.

&   Spending Money

How much money we spend, how often we spend it, and what we spend it on can become a source of conflict in a marriage. Again, open discussion about your values and history can help you understand each other. Identify what each partner *needs* versus what each person *wants*. If money is short, you may need to restrict most expenditures to necessities and find ways to fill the "wants" with extra income or gift money. Talk about patterns of spending and what emotional needs may be met by various spending habits. Remember that filling emotional needs is not necessarily bad; it is only problematic if it is excessive or creates conflict in your relationship. If not, you may simply agree that buying cookbooks when you are depressed (Linda's emotional fix!) is affordable and even somewhat useful.

Spending patterns obviously become a problem whenever your expenditures exceed your income. Careful analysis of how you spend your money, along with reflection on why you spend it, can often help you decide how to cut expenditures. Obviously, this assumes that both partners know all sources of income and all expenditures and are willing to discuss them openly and honestly. Where there are differences, listen carefully to each other and negotiate solutions that you can try and later evaluate to see if they succeeded.

One way to begin getting runaway spending habits under control is to make a record of each and every expenditure, along with notes about how you felt at the time and why you were making that purchase. Many people discover that this analysis helps them see where they are spending money without realizing it and what emotional triggers may be influencing their purchases. Try recording everything you spend and labelling each item as Necessary, Useful, Wanted, or Luxury. Then review your notes to see what you can learn about your spending patterns.

ﾌ Borrowing Money

One of the most seductive features of money today is the ease with which it can be borrowed. This is especially true for credit cards. In fact, people have noticed that if they have a large credit card balance, they can be assured of more credit card offers with spending levels increased from those they already have, even if they have a relatively low income or are already overextended. Many people find themselves deep in debt before they realize they are in trouble.

Some people have no idea how much they owe or how much interest they pay for the debt they carry. It is important that you regularly review your total debt obligations (home mortgages, credit cards, car, school, and personal loans) and assess whether that debt is benefiting you or hurting you. Add up the amount of monthly interest for each loan and credit card and project that into the future (one year, five years, ten years) to see what your debts are costing. Then decide if that cost is worthwhile. Careful control of your debts will, in the end, give you more money to spend.

Finally, there is the question of whom you will ask for a loan. Credit cards companies offer their services often. Banks are usually fairly strict and rarely make personal loans that exceed your capacity to repay them. Local "loan sharks" will give you what you want but will charge you excessively high interest and may be quite unpleasant about collecting what you owe them. Failure to repay any of these lenders usually results in repossession of items, legal action, and/or a negative credit record.

Many couples find themselves, especially in the early years of marriage, turning to parents, other relatives, or friends as sources of money with no credit check and low or no interest payments. The problem is that they can lend you more money than you can afford to repay. They also may assume that loaning you money gives them the right to dictate how it is spent. So, your parents may lend you money to buy furniture, but then criticize what you buy or feel free to comment on other expenditures. Money is power, and borrowing money from friends and family usually affects the balance of power in those relationships—which may affect your marriage as well.

> ### Major Indebtedness
>
> If you are preparing for marriage and one or both of you has a large debt, you need to discuss the debt before you marry. Develop a budget for repaying the debt and discuss how you feel about living within those constraints. Be aware of the lifestyle changes that may be required and decide if the potential strain on your relationship is worth choosing to marry now; if not, find a way to reduce or eliminate the debt first. In particular, develop a strategy to handle the debt if one or both of you were to die immediately after the wedding.
>
> If you are already married and have large debts, you may find it helpful to talk with a financial advisor. This will be necessary if you are experiencing financial difficulties and have been unable to resolve them. Managing a large debt load can put a strain on any marriage. Seek assistance and make the necessary adjustments to enable you to handle the debt comfortably. Again, make provisions for what will happen if one or both of you were to die.

If you choose to borrow from a friend or relative, we urge you to treat the loan in the same manner as you would if you were borrowing from strangers. Make sure you can repay it and work out a clear repayment plan. Add interest—paying for the use of the money helps restore the balance of power. If it is a significant sum, put it in writing and make your payments faithfully.

Sometimes these loans work very well; sometimes they create enormous difficulties. Plan for what you will do if difficulties arise. If you borrow amounts that are reasonable, for example, you might be able to go to a commercial lender, borrow the money you need, and repay the family member or friend and thus remove the difficulties. Take care not to sacrifice significant relationships for the sake of money.

ಐ Saving Money

Saving money is not valued highly today. When interest rates are low, it is easier to justify spending whatever we have. It is only when you look at the interest you pay when you must borrow money that saving becomes attractive. It is looking *far* into the future that makes saving important.

"Pay yourself first" is the old adage, and it is worth heeding. No matter how low your income, try to set aside some fixed amount from every paycheck. If you do that from the day you get married, it will become a habit and you will automatically adjust your lifestyle to adapt to it. Making saving a habit makes it easier. If you decide to save for purchases now and the future, you may want to set up two accounts: a *spend now/emergency* savings account that you periodically use for major purchases, and a *retirement* savings account that you do not touch. Remember, many companies will match your contribution to a savings plan if you choose to deduct it from your salary and sometimes they set up tax deferred plans as well. Electing to participate in such a plan is the easiest way to give yourself a raise!

ಐ Lending Money

At some point (perhaps hard to anticipate now!) you may have enough money to lend to others. Usually the request for a loan will come from your children, family members, friends, or co-workers. Sometimes that request will come when you don't have enough money to go around. Often it will come with emotional "hooks" that generate feelings of guilt or obligation.

As a couple, it is our principle never to lend money with the expectation of return. We don't say that to the borrower, but if we can't afford to lose the money, we don't lend it. Lending money to someone who does not repay you often damages or even destroys the relationship, especially if it is a close friend or family member. So, if we are going to lend money, we choose to see it as a gift. If it ever returns, fine. We see that repaid loan as a gift to us and use it for luxury items or give it away again.

If you have several people who frequently ask you for money, you may want to set a "norm" so you don't have to decide what to do each time and so the person who is asking doesn't feel singled out. Then, for example, you can say: "We have decided that we will not loan money to anyone" or "We've decided to set $100 as the limit we will lend anyone." Discuss and decide in advance if, when, and to whom you will lend money and then stick to that agreement. If you have decided not to loan money and one of you is much better at saying "no" than the other, that person may choose to be the bearer of bad news. If you choose to lend significant sums of money it is usually best to put the terms in writing.

What is important in lending money is that the two of you decide together what you will do and that you resist the often inevitable pressures from others and the emotional pressures from within. Most difficulties around lending money come when we end up doing what we really don't want to do.

❧ Giving Money Away

Throughout your marriage there will be many occasions when you will be asked to give money to a variety of worthy causes. Again, the two of you may have different values about giving and different approaches to when, where, and to whom you give. Understanding your history and discussing your values can help you decide how you will give to others.

The Widow's Mite

Jesus sat down opposite the treasury, and watched the crowd putting money into the treasury. Many rich people put in large sums. A poor widow came and put in two small copper coins, which are worth a penny. Then he called his disciples and said to them, "Truly I tell you, this poor widow has put in more than all those who are contributing to the treasury. For all of them have contributed out of their abundance; but she out of her poverty has put in everything she had, all she had to live on." (Mark 12:41-44; see also Luke 21:1-4)

What does this story say to you about giving? In the United States, poor people consistently give a greater percentage of their income than rich people. Why do you think this is true? Why do people give to others? Why do you give?

The Christian faith encourages us to give to others both as a way to "love one another" and because giving to others is a way we give thanks for what we have received. Just writing a check rarely does that. But giving ourselves—our time, our skills, our support, our participation *and* our money—becomes a thank offering. Often we think that we can get by with just giving our "time and talent"; God calls us to give our treasure as well. Good stewardship means using all the resources we have been given wisely—for our good and for the good of others.

& Receiving Money from Others

It seems hard to imagine that receiving money could be anything but a good thing. Yet consider how many marriages come apart after someone wins millions in the lottery or is the beneficiary of an inheritance. More common are the problems that come when someone, usually parents, give money as a gift, with or without strings attached.

Just like borrowing money, receiving money can tip the balance of power. Someone who gives money may expect something in return—love, time with you, your attention, or the acceptance of their advice. Often those expectations are unconscious, but the impact on your relationship may be profound. Sometimes there are no expectations from the giver, but you create them yourself. You may feel obligated and then may become burdened by and angry about that sense of obligation. Or, you may feel guilty about accepting money instead of earning it. If family money is distributed unequally, it often creates family rifts and may cause you much discomfort, whether you're the one getting the most or the least. Money has a strange way of creating strong feelings and distorting relationships. When monetary gifts become destructive to your relationship you need to find a way to remove that negative impact, even if that means refusing to accept the money.

Plan for unexpected windfalls, too. It may just be a nice fantasy, but if you've had some discussion about what you would do with a large amount of extra money you'll have a head start on becoming aware of any major differences in how the two of you would handle a windfall. Your discussion will also give you valuable clues about how each of you feels about any amount of extra money. And that is, of course, where most of us will actually face our differences.

& Making Provision for Others

Finally, there is the matter of leaving your money to others when you die. Couples planning a wedding rarely, if ever, think about what might happen if one or both of them died on the honeymoon or shortly thereafter. Who will pay the debts? Who will inherit the property? Those in the first few years of marriage and even those married for a long time also often ignore these questions. (This certainly applies to us—we're in the midst of doing this some years after our wedding!)

Many people assume their property will automatically go to their spouse. In some states and in certain cases that is true. But if you die without a will, the distribution may depend on whose names are on the accounts and what rules govern the state or province in which you reside. You may be surprised to discover that money you thought would go to your spouse is divided between your spouse and children, or that a portion goes to your parents or other "next of kin." In addition, the costs of settling the estate under these circumstances will increase significantly. Individual as well as joint debts may become the responsibility of the remaining spouse (including business or other debts of which you may not be aware).

Discussing all these details and making the appropriate legal arrangements is important to do, even in the midst of a very busy time. Making these plans becomes *especially* important if you have children. Talk with a lawyer about drafting a will, setting up trust agreements, and obtaining appropriate insurance protection shortly before or immediately after the wedding. If you are already married and have not made these arrangements, do so as soon as possible. Then update those arrangements regularly.

ᴥ "I Honor You"

During the exchange of rings in the marriage service each partner tells the other, "with all that I am, and all that I have, I honor you" (BCP 427). What does it mean

---

Disposing of our Temporal Goods

In the Episcopal Church the only clear instruction we have on the distribution of our possessions comes in a rubric for the service of Thanksgiving for the Birth or Adoption of a Child:

The Minister of the Congregations is directed in instruct the people, from time to time, about the duty of Christian parents to make prudent provisions for the well-being of their families, and of all persons to make wills, while they are in health, arranging for the disposal of their temporal goods, not neglecting, if they are able, to leave bequests for religious and charitable uses. (BCP 445)

Many clergy are uncomfortable giving this instruction because it feels like they are asking for money. Why do you think this instruction is in the prayer book? What value does it have for the congregation? for the individual members of the congregation? How might churches help members fulfill their responsibilities in making provision for their families and for future generations of Christians?

to honor another person with all that we are and have? To honor someone means to have esteem for them, to respect them, even to reverence them ("to have profound awe and respect and often love").

When we marry we make a commitment to participate in the process of entrusting all of ourselves to our partner. That doesn't happen instantly, when we say the words at the altar. It occurs over the months and years of living together and sharing our being and our possessions. Many couples begin life together with separate checking and savings accounts, loans and vehicle titles in one partner's name, and a clear sense of "what's mine" and "what's yours." Almost immediately they acquire possessions that are "ours"—wedding gifts, for example. Soon a rental lease or home mortgage is in both names. But at some point the couple needs to deal with whether they will live in a "mine, yours, ours" world or if there will be just "ours."

This shift may be very difficult for some people. As we have said, in our culture money represents power, security, and identity. So it is understandable that many of us find it difficult to give another person total access to the money we earn or to give up our sense of sole ownership of a car, furniture, or other favored possession. Yet marriage is a partnership in which "the two shall become one." It is when we fully share all that we are and have that this becomes a reality. Our lives and our fortunes become interdependent.

Learning to live interdependently, to share what we have and to care for

> ### *Our Heart's Desire*
>
> *Do not store up for yourselves treasures on earth, where moth and rust consume and where thieves break in and steal; but store up for yourselves treasures in heaven, where neither moth nor rust consumes and where thieves do not break in and steal. For where your treasure is, there your heart will be also.* (Matt. 6:19-21)
>
> What do you treasure? What is your heart's desire?
>
> Jesus knew the potential for good or ill in the relationship between people and money. One-sixth of his words and one-third of his parables are about money. To Jesus, money, more than anything else, had the potential to deepen or destroy one's relationship with God. What we earn, how we think about our money, and how we use our possessions affects who we are.

one another, is part of the Christian's spiritual journey. We are not the owners of our money or possessions; we are the stewards of them. They have been entrusted to our care and we are ultimately accountable to God for our stewardship of all that is given to us. Making careful and prayerful decisions about money—what we choose to buy with it and how we care for those possessions—helps us become faithful stewards.

The question is not just "What do I want?" or even "What do *we* want?" The question is much broader: How does our use of the resources given to us become "a sign of Christ's love to this sinful and broken world" (BCP 429)?

Possessions—or the money we use to buy them—can become our primary purpose in life. They can occupy our time and attention in buying them, caring for them, safeguarding them, and showcasing them. Possessions we want but don't have can capture our imagination, permeate our dreams, and drive our ambitions. Instead of being the stewards of our possessions we become possessed by them.

We can choose to be stewards instead, to value, respect, and care for what we have with the understanding that all things come from and belong to God. We may have earned the money, but we cannot earn our life, our body and brains, our talents and skills, the raw materials of the earth, and the countless opportunities to learn, grow, and develop as people: these are given. Each of us has been given a set of these resources with the expectation that we will be trustworthy custodians of them.

The marriage relationship is a place where we can take what we have been given and care for it, preserve it, use it, develop it, and produce something of value or of beauty from it: a product, a service, a better person, a deeper relationship. Whatever we have, whatever we create, we do so with the gifts given us by a God who loves us and wants the best for us. We are called to responsible living in community. Our decisions about money and possessions are not just personal; they affect each other, our families, the larger community, and our relationship with God.

> # QUESTIONS FOR COUPLES
> # TO DISCUSS

☙ Marriage Preparation

- What was your family's level of income? What was their attitude toward money? How might this affect your marriage?

- What has been your personal experience with money? What would you identify as your strengths and your weaknesses in handling money?

- How much money do each of you earn? How much do you expect to make in the next year? five years? ten years? How much do you expect your partner to make? What if you make less? more? How do you feel about your partner making more money than you? less money than you?

- What assets do you have: physical (car, house, furniture, jewelry) and monetary (cash, investments, trust funds, stocks)?

- What has been your past and present experience with and feelings about spending and saving? Are those patterns significantly different from your partner's? If so, how will you deal with those differences?

- What indebtedness do you have (car, house, school loans, credit cards, personal loans)? What loans have you made to others?

- What has been your past and presence experience with and feelings about debt? about loaning money to others? Are those patterns significantly different from your partner's? If so, how will you deal with those differences? Do you anticipate borrowing money in the next year or two? If so, from whom, for what, and how much?

- Have you ever gambled? If so, how frequently? How much do you bet and in what contexts? Do you have any compulsive tendencies? Have you ever had any problems (fights, arrests, debts) due to gambling?

- What insurance policies do you have? What policies will you need (life, health, dental, vision, house, car)?

- What do you anticipate you would do with an inheritance, lottery winnings, insurance settlement, or other windfall?

- What plans do you have for savings? investments? pensions? Are those plans significantly different from your partner's? If so, how will you deal with those differences?

- How much do you now give to others? When, how, and to whom? How much do you think you will give when you are married? How do you want to make those decisions?

- What arrangements have you made or do you plan to make for leaving your possessions to others after you die? Have you or will you include bequests to the church or other charitable organizations? Why or why not?

- If one or both of you died on your honeymoon, who would get your money and possessions? If one of you were left alone, would your assets and insurance enable that person to live without undue hardship? If either of you has children, who would raise them? Would your assets and insurance provide adequately for them?

- How do you manage your checkbook, pay bills, do the banking, make investment decisions? How do you want to handle those tasks when you are married? How often will you communicate about money (daily, weekly, monthly, or when a crisis arises)?

- What is your pattern of communication about money now? What does that tell you about how you will communicate later? What changes might you want to make?

- What did you learn from this chapter? What decisions do you choose to make in response to what you learned?

Ȣ Marriage Enrichment

- What connections do you see between your family's way of handling money and their attitude toward money, and how you manage money in your marriage? How have you handled any significant differences in your background or prior lifestyle or any difficulties around money you've encountered in your marriage thus far?

- What has been your personal experience with money? What would you identify as your strengths and your weaknesses in handling money?

- How do you manage your checkbook, pay bills, do the banking, make investment decisions? How often do you communicate as a couple about money (daily, weekly, monthly, or when a crisis arises)? Are you comfortable with this arrangement? What changes, if any, would you like to make in the way money is managed in your marriage?

- What patterns of spending, saving, earning, borrowing, loaning, and giving money do you see in your marriage? Have any of these patterns been a source of discomfort or conflict in your marriage?

- How much money do each of you earn? How much do you expect to make in the next year? five years? ten years? How much do you expect your spouse to make? What if you make less? more? How do you feel about your spouse making more money than you? less money than you?

- Would you be able to list what assets you have, both physical (car, house, furniture, jewelery) and monetary (cash, investments, trust funds, stocks)? Do you know what indebtedness you have (car, house, school loans, credit cards, personal loans)? Can you find out how much annual interest you pay for each of those debts and what loans you've made to others?

- What insurance policies do you have? Are they adequate for your needs? Do each of you have a will or trust fund? When did you last review and update them? Do you know where important documents—insurance policies, wills, lists of bank accounts, trust documents, real estate deeds, vehicle titles, safe deposit box number—are kept? Are the names of the owners, executors, beneficiaries, and terms of each accurate and adequate?

- What do you anticipate you would do with an inheritance, lottery winnings, insurance settlement, or other windfall?

- What plans do you have for retirement? What investments do you have? pensions? When did you last review and update your plans? Are you implementing those plans consistently? What changes, if any, would you like to make?

- How much money do you give to others? When, how, and to whom do you give? Are you comfortable with the way you make those decisions? What arrangements have you made for leaving your possessions to others after you die? Have you included bequests to the church or other charitable organizations? Why or why not?

- What did you learn from this chapter? What decisions do you choose to make in response to what you learned?

> # QUESTIONS FOR GROUPS
> # TO DISCUSS

- Do you know of marriages that have been significantly affected by money? Have you heard of or seen marriages destroyed by money? What role do you think money played? What do you think a couple can do to keep money from having a negative impact on their marriage?

- How did your family of origin deal with money issues? How has that affected your relationship? What are some ways couples can handle the negative impact on their marriage?

- How do you handle money? Who pays the bills, balances the checkbook, makes investment decisions? What are some helpful ways couples can work together to manage their financial affairs?

- How do you handle differences in spending and saving habits? How might couples handle differences or difficulties they encounter around spending and saving?

- How do you handle differences in habits concerning borrowing and debt management? How might couples handle differences or difficulties they encounter around borrowing money?

- How do you feel about borrowing from or lending money to family, friends or co-workers? How do you feel about receiving money from them? What problems can you anticipate and what strategies would you have to deal with them?

- When did you last do any kind of budgeting or financial analysis? Why is budgeting and reviewing finances important?

- Why is it important to give to others? How do you/will you handle contributions in your marriage?

- Discuss the issue of making wills, setting up trust funds for children, obtaining insurance, and otherwise making plans for the future and for your death. Have you made these provisions? How do you feel about making them? What do they have to do with marriage?

- Discuss how you feel about leaving bequests to the church or other charitable organizations.

- What is your understanding of "stewardship" or "responsible living in community"? How will you make good stewardship a part of your daily life?

- What did you learn from this chapter? What decisions do you choose to make in response to what you learned?

SUGGESTED PROJECTS

- Prepare an analysis of your current financial situation. Make a His, Hers, and Combined list for each of the following items, with total amount and payoff or receipt dates where applicable.

  ASSETS: cash, savings accounts, stocks, bonds, CDs, pension/retirement funds, trust funds, cash-value life insurance, other investments, jewelry, vehicles, furniture, artwork, appliances, real estate, clothing, insurance settlements you expect to receive, expected inheritance, loans you expect will be repaid, tax refunds you expect, child support, alimony, other assets.

  LIABILITIES: loans (car, home, school, personal, business, other), credit cards, lines of credit, child support, alimony, taxes you owe (back taxes or if not withheld), unpaid bills, other liabilities.

- Using your analysis of your current financial situation, prepare a joint budget for the first months or next few months of your marriage. Include the following items in your monthly budget (pro-rate annual expenses).

  INCOME: take-home salaries, bonuses, interest income, dividends, sale of assets, child support, alimony, rental income, trust income, royalties, gifts, other income.

  EXPENSES: mortgage/rent, property tax, insurance, maintenance fee/repairs, home improvements, utilities, phone, home decorating (furniture, art, painting), appliances, miscellaneous, vehicle payments, gas/oil, vehicle repairs, vehicle insurance, license fees, parking, public transportation, groceries, liquor/beer/tobacco, personal care items, medical/dental/vision, drugs/medicine, eating out, movies/videos, newspapers, magazines, cable television, computer networks, books, clothes, cleaning, hobbies, sports/cultural events, other entertainment, health/dental/vision insurance, life insurance, personal retirement savings (not by employer), income/Social Security/Medicare taxes (not withheld), alimony, child support, child care, savings, pets, education expenses, contributions, gifts, memberships/subscriptions, vacations, personal allowances (his, hers, children).

- Discuss how this process of analyzing and developing financial plans felt. Was it difficult or easy, what you expected or a surprise? What did you learn?

Sexual Intimacy

The union of husband and wife in heart, body, and mind is
intended by God for their mutual joy...for the help and comfort
they give one another...for the procreation of children.
(BCP 423)

"Most couples engage in premarital sex."
"Couples today spend most of their honeymoon in bed."
"Sex in the early days is frequent and passionate."
"Most people have good sex naturally and always find it enjoyable."
"Sexual inhibitions are outdated."
These and many other assumptions people make about sex are simply wrong. There are still people who do not engage in premarital sex or who have far less sexual experience than we might expect. After a long, stressful service, dinner, dance, and travel, many honeymooners are in bed—sleeping! Some people find their sex lives disappointing or even uncomfortable; many are not as uninhibited as we might guess.

We live in a time after the "sexual revolution" when inhibitions and restrictions on sex supposedly were overthrown. We live in a society permeated with messages about sex, most of which focus on looking good, feeling good, and being good in bed. We live in a culture that equates sexual intimacy with intercourse. All these things help make sex a bit more complicated than "just doing it."

ဆ What is Sexual Intimacy?

Sexual intimacy is more than just having intercourse. It's even more than foreplay and afterplay. Sexual intimacy includes all the words and actions we do to build a level of intimacy that engages our whole being—body, mind, and spirit. It has been said that sexuality and spirituality are very close to each other. Both of them engage us completely. In both our sexual lives and our spiritual lives the deepest, most intimate, and truest parts of ourselves are opened to another. In spirituality that "other" is God; in sexuality it is our partner. In the sexual intimacy of marriage, it is both. We open ourselves, make ourselves totally vulnerable to our partner, and in that meeting of body, mind, and soul, we meet God and each other.

The mechanics of sex are the easy part! Completely trusting yourself to another person and to God is much more difficult. The act of giving ourselves to another reveals and conveys who we are completely in ways that allow us to be vulnerable and authentic. Because of this, sexual intimacy is the most powerful form of communication possible between two people. The physical union of a couple is an expression and a symbol of the intimacy between them; no greater form of intimacy between two people is possible. While we may share experiences and confidences with family members and friends, nothing compares with this closeness.

Sexuality is a sacred gift from God. The sexual drive is a powerful force; through it life is created and sustained. Its force and power are not to be taken lightly, but must be respected. The sexual drive is combined with a depth of self-giving and self-revelation to create sexual intimacy. That intimacy forms a sacred bond between husband and wife that must be protected. If that bond is broken, a sacred trust is violated.

Developing sexual intimacy takes time. Most people do not immediately and automatically trust their whole being to another person. The experience of falling in love helps us do that. But over time, the initial psychological dynamics of falling in love diminish. We begin to see our loved one in a different light. The idealized lover we created in our minds becomes more realistic as we face that person day after day. Often the passionate sexual activity that goes with making love with our idealized lover begins to change even as our relationship with our loved one changes. As we gradually reveal ourselves as we really are, our sexual relationship moves to a new level. Over time our sexual intimacy is deepened. The capacity for deepening that intimacy is endless, but it doesn't happen magically, all by itself.

౭౨ The 20:1 Ratio

There is a common sense norm that says a healthy relationship needs twenty "strokes" for every negative. That's twenty hugs, kisses, compliments, smiles, winks, cuddles, little favors, affirmations, affectionate glances, private nicknames, "I love you's," jokes, thank you's, attentive listenings, nips at the back of the neck, backrubs, steamy showers, or heartfelt "you're wonderful's" for every snide remark. Or **every** angry outburst. Or every cold shoulder.

The way you deepen sexual intimacy is to nourish your relationship daily, with lots of loving strokes. Sexual intimacy is expressed in a hundred different ways. Just having intercourse can get mechanical and meaningless. What makes it enjoyable is all the hundreds of little things we do all day, every day that build our relationship and intimacy. Part of being married is taking the time to do those twenty strokes for every negative. And part of it is knowing that the two of you will be around long enough to build a relationship that is deeper and broader than just intercourse.

In his book *Praying Shapes Believing,* Lee Mitchell notes that what we say and what we do in liturgy (worship) shapes what we believe. Many social scientists say the opposite—that what we believe shapes how we behave. Together they tell us that there is a relationship between what we believe internally and how we behave (what we say and do). When love begins, that relationship between beliefs and behavior is obvious—"I love you, therefore I do and say loving things." But when years go by and conflicts arise, you may begin to wonder—"I don't do or say loving things; do I still love you?" Even before those doubts creep in, many couples discover that the sexual relationship begins to reflect the distance growing between the couple.

When that happens it is a clear signal that the two of you have not given adequate attention to your love relationship. To renew your love you need to change what you believe and/or how you behave. You can pick either believing *or* doing as a starting point. Begin doing or saying lov-

> ### Saying "I Love You"
>
> In the beginning it is easy and natural for most people to say "I love you" often and with feeling. After awhile many people begin to assume their partner knows they are loved and they stop saying "I love you" on a regular basis. Saying "I love you" is important because it does more than send information: it both expresses and shapes our beliefs about ourselves and each other.
>
> A marriage counselor once said that saying "I love you" five times a day is the secret to a good marriage. While those three words are not a magic incantation, saying them is more important than their size would indicate. Find times and ways to say "I love you" to each other. It can't hurt, and it probably helps more than we want to admit!

ing things. Or begin thinking loving thoughts. Constantly telling yourself that you no longer find your spouse attractive or that you don't love him or her anymore discourages you from doing or saying things that build up the relationship. Failing to do and say loving things regularly eventually undermines your belief that you love each other and becomes a self-perpetuating cycle until you have quietly killed your love.

You can choose to act differently and discover that being a loving partner fuels love. You can choose to think differently and discover that believing you love your partner fuels love. You can choose to create a positive cycle as easily as a negative cycle. What you think/believe and what you say/do have an impact on each other. Both are important. Thinking, saying, and doing those things that create and fuel love builds sexual intimacy. When you are in love, you do that naturally. When things are not going well, it takes a conscious choice to make the extra effort required. Usually the restoration of the positive cycle of thinking/believing and saying/doing loving things also restores a positive sexual relationship.

෨ Good Sex, Bad Sex

It is surprising how many people have sexual relationships that are disappointing, discomforting, or even disagreeable. If this is true for you now or fear it will be true in the future, you are not alone! Nor do you have to live with it.

If you're disappointed, you may be able to resolve the issue by doing a reality check—our expectations, fuelled by societal myths, sometimes exceed human capacities! If your expectations are realistic but you aren't sexually satisfied, good communication may resolve the problem. The most common sexual difficulty is that we think our partner can read our minds! We assume that what satisfies us is obvious when, in reality, people's sexual needs and preferences are quite different. There simply is no way for your partner to know what works for you without your communicating that indirectly (by showing pleasure when he or she happens to do the right thing) or directly (by telling your partner what you don't like and what you enjoy).

If you are normally reticent about discussing your sexual desires, take courage in hand and do so anyway. Before you begin, make sure both of you understand that it is extremely important that you listen with respect and do not make fun of or express disgust or disdain for each other's preferences. Expressing a sexual preference is fine even if you choose not to engage in that specific activity. Discuss and try whatever seems right to the two of you.

While it is appropriate for you to do what is enjoyable and agreeable *to the two of you* it is also possible that some things may not be enjoyable or agreeable *to one of you*. If that is true for you, say "no" to that activity. Some people will agree to do something they don't particularly enjoy (but don't find especially disagreeable)

Sexual Abuse

A sexual relationship in which one partner manipulates, pressures, or forces the other to do things he or she doesn't freely choose to do is not healthy and is, in fact, abusive. No one, not even your spouse, has the right to demand that you do something against your will.

Most people know when they are being manipulated, pressured, or forced, but many do not readily admit it, even to themselves. Some points to help you decide if you need to seek help for abuse, sexual difficulties, or other problems include:

- If your relationship is seriously imbalanced: your partner greatly enjoys sex while you don't; you always do what your partner wants and rarely, if ever, do what you want or need.

- If you consistently feel depressed, nauseated, or angry after sex.

- If you are engaged in sex with more than one person or in settings that make you feel afraid or ashamed.

If you find yourself in any of these situations, seek help from a professional counselor. As with physical abuse, sexual abuse needs to be addressed promptly. Remember, *do not accept abuse from anyone at anytime.*

because they want to please their partner and they find his or her pleasure enjoyable. That's fine. But doing something you find disagreeable or feeling pressured to do something you really don't want to do will not help your sex life or your relationship. Again, talking to each other is important so you can be clear that saying "no" to some specific activity does not mean saying "no" to loving your partner. A couple with a healthy relationship will not engage in sexual activities that make one of them feel uncomfortable, disgusted, or afraid, or that causes pain.

Finally, at some point you may experience sexual dysfunction—impotence, severe pain, obvious emotional distress, or something that is so uncomfortable you choose not to engage in sex at all or only infrequently. You may find the very idea of sex unpleasant. These problems can have a physical or emotional basis. In either case, you may want to consult with a physician (to rule out a physical cause) and you may choose to pursue therapy. If the problem is relatively minor (occasional impotence, for example), you may want to try some of the better self-help books on the market. If it is situational (loss of sexual interest in a time of high stress), just waiting it out may help. Often sexual problems can be resolved with time, patience, and some tender, loving care.

∞ Seeking Help for Sexual Problems

An enjoyable sexual relationship is an important part of a happy, healthy marriage, yet because sex is such a private matter, many people are reluctant to seek help when they encounter sexual difficulties. If you are encountering general sexual difficulties that time, discussion, reading books, and tender, loving care don't resolve, we encourage you to take courage and find someone trained to help with sexual problems.

There are some specific situations that may contribute to sexual difficulties and generally require some help from a counselor. If one or both of you have experienced rape, incest, or sexual abuse (as victim or perpetrator), it is highly likely that the experience will have an impact on your sexual relationship. Unless you have already received counseling and/or have "worked through" your experience, it would be helpful to seek professional help. Ignoring traumatic incidents such as these does not make them go away. It is important that you address them and have the support and help you need to face the pain, anger, guilt, and other powerful effects of such experiences. If you do not do so, those feelings will seep out and poison your sexual relationship, and can ultimately undermine your marriage.

If you are a victim or perpetrator of rape, incest, or sexual abuse and have not told your partner about this before now, it would be helpful to discuss the matter with your clergyperson and/or a professional counselor before you decide to do so.

High-risk Behaviors and Sexual Addictions

Have you ever participated in behaviors such as prostitution, exhibitionism, voyeurism, anonymous sex, pedophilia (sex with children), incestuous relationships, group sex, bestiality, or other sexual addictions? If you have engaged in some high-risk behaviors *even one time* you may have the HIV virus or a sexually transmitted disease (STD), even if you have no symptoms. High-risk behaviors include any unprotected intercourse (heterosexual or homosexual), oral or anal sex, sharing needles or syringes, and receiving a blood transfusion before 1985.

You may have an obligation to tell your spouse or partner that you have engaged in addictive or high-risk behaviors in the past, especially if you have HIV/AIDS or a sexually transmitted disease, unless you did so many years ago and have since had at least two tests (six months apart) indicating that you were not infected. If you have HIV/AIDS or a STD and have not yet discussed it with your partner, your doctor and/or a counselor can help you decide how to do that and can support you and your partner in making appropriate health decisions. You may wish to discuss any sexual addictions with a counselor before discussing them with your partner.

A counselor can help you decide if, when, where, and how to tell your partner about the experience. You may need support in discussing the situation and a counselor can help you think about how you can tell your story in a way which builds rather than hurts your relationship. A counselor can also help your partner deal with his or her reaction to your story.

If you have had an abortion in the past, you may find that it has an impact on your sexual relationship. If you later encounter sexual difficulties, your partner's support and understanding will be important in overcoming those problems. It may be difficult for him to understand what is happening if he does not know about your abortion and your feelings about it.

Again, it would be very helpful to discuss this with a counselor before you decide if or how you will tell your partner about this experience. Some women who have

---

On Childbirth and Abortion

General Convention, the legislative body of the Episcopal Church, adopts resolutions designed to help its members make decisions. The following is the resolution on abortion.

All life is sacred. Hence, it is sacred from its inception until death. The Church takes seriously its obligation to help form the consciences of its members concerning this sacredness. Human life, therefore, should be initiated only advisedly and in full accord with this understanding of the power to conceive and give birth which is bestowed by God....

We regard all abortion as having a tragic dimension, calling for the concern and compassion of all the Christian community.

While we acknowledge that in this country it is the legal right of every woman to have a medically safe abortion, as Christians we believe strongly that if this right is exercised, it should be used only in extreme situations. We emphatically oppose abortion as a means of birth control, family planning, sex selection, or any reason of mere convenience....

Whenever members of this Church are consulted with regard to a problem pregnancy, they are to explore, with grave seriousness, with the person or persons seeking advice and counsel, as alternatives to abortion, other positive courses of action, including, but not limited to, the following possibilities: the parents raising the child; another family member raising the child; making the child available for adoption.

— Resolution C047a, *Journal of the General Convention,* 1988

had abortions and did not have any negative reaction or have resolved those feelings may choose to leave that experience in the past. You need to consider the impact of telling your partner now versus the impact of telling him later or perhaps having him learn about it from someone else.

Of course, you may also face the question of abortion if you conceive a child whom you feel unable to bear. This is an extremely difficult decision for anyone to make alone. The church provides its members with general guidance regarding abortion but also makes it clear that those considering abortion should seek the advice, counsel, and support of other Christians.

We feel we need to offer a few cautionary words about discussing sexual matters with others—even with professionals and clergy. Most people have *very strong* feelings about subjects such as abortion, AIDS, extramarital affairs, homosexuality, and other sexual matters. They may *aggressively* advocate for or against certain behaviors and become very critical of those holding another viewpoint or engaging in those behaviors. Discussing these subjects *on an abstract level* with such a person may be informative, challenging, and even fun. Discussing them with such a person when you are in emotional pain or trying to make a decision is not helpful and may be harmful.

If you find yourself in a situation where your counselor is derogatory or mean, state (if you can) what effect his or her behavior is having on you and then leave. Find someone else who can listen and be supportive. You and your counselor do not have to agree, but the person helping you should not exhibit any aggressive or abusive behaviors, no matter how strongly he or she may feel about a subject. Do not accept counseling from anyone who is abusive.

Finding Help in the Church

If you need assistance in finding someone in the church who could help you concerning sexual difficulties in your marriage, ask your clergyperson or a trusted lay person who knows the diocesan clergy. Or call your bishop's office, name the topic you want to discuss, and ask for a referral to a clergyperson who can help you in a supportive fashion. You do not have to leave your full name; your first name and a phone number is adequate for them to respond to your request. Most clergy and diocesan offices we know will help you find a supportive person.

Finally, and sadly, we need to say that discussing sexual difficulties of any sort can create an environment in which you become vulnerable to sexual misconduct on the part of the counselor. *No sexual problem is ever solved by having the counselor and counseled person engage in sexual activity with each other.* If anyone suggests this, leave immediately and contact the appropriate authorities (bishop, police, professional association). Also, be aware of excessively detailed questions about your sexual activities. Clergy, in particular, are rarely trained to deal with sexual dysfunction and so do not need to hear any details. Requests for details are inappropriate. Again, leave immediately and discuss your concerns with the appropriate persons.

Most dioceses have a sexual misconduct process in place to handle complaints about clergy and laity employed by the church—call your bishop's office for information on whom to contact. Concerns about members of your congregation should be discussed with your clergyperson as soon as possible. Your clergyperson can also help you identify the appropriate professional association or agencies that should be contacted if you experience problems with a counselor not associated with the church.

о The Purpose of Sex

In the "old days" the church declared that the purpose of sex was the procreation of children. Period. No fun and games. Nothing about love and pleasure. Just do it to make babies. Many people think that is still the position of the church.

> ### Enjoying Sex
>
> There are a host of books, videos, and programs that can help you discover a thousand and one different ways to enjoy sex. Go ahead and buy some of them! Read, watch, and have your horizons expanded. But above all, play a little. Our culture is a bit too serious at times. Sex is fun, and it is more fun when you can learn to play. Don't worry so much about getting your performance right—just enjoy!

Fortunately, times have changed and the church now acknowledges other purposes of sex alongside the procreative. The marriage service states that "the union of husband and wife in heart, body, and mind is intended by God for their mutual joy" (BCP 423). The Canadian marriage service is even clearer: "The union of man and woman in heart, body, and mind is intended for their mutual comfort and help, that they may know each other with delight and tenderness in acts of love" (BAS 528).

While creating life is an important reason to have a sexual relationship, it is not the only reason. As those who have been together for many years know, a good sexual relationship provides help, comfort, and mutual joy. Trusting another human being with all that we are, making ourselves completely open and vulnerable and being completely accepted is indeed a source of great joy.

ം Make Time for Sex

Those who are preparing for marriage or are newly married may find this injunction strange. Those who have been married awhile probably know that familiarity and the demands of daily life (especially if you have a demanding career or children) eat up most of your time and energy. Time just for the two of you tends to diminish or even disappear.

It is crucial for your marriage that you consistently arrange times when just the two of you can be together. You don't have to make love during that time, but you do need to have the time and space to express love. Some of that time might be short and daily—a few minutes of snuggle time before bed or in the morning. Some of it might be weekly—on Friday nights get a babysitter and go dancing. Some of it might be occasionally—a special night or weekend away. Best is a regular combination of daily, weekly, and occasional times for just you.

A sexual relationship, like any relationship, takes time to build. Spend time flirting and courting each other. Because our sexuality and our spirituality are so closely related, spending time building sexual intimacy with our partner contributes to building our spiritual life as well. Moving beyond mere intercourse to being deeply and fully "at one" with our partner brings us into that space where, at some deep level, we are aware of being "at one" with God. In eastern cultures people bow to one another as a way of saying "the sacred in me bows to the sacred in you." In the fullest sexual union of body, mind, and soul, the sacred in me meets the sacred in you.

QUESTIONS FOR COUPLES TO DISCUSS

ဆ Marriage Preparation

- What events or attitudes from your family of origin or your past experience have influenced your sexual behaviors and feelings? How have you dealt with those experiences or attitudes that have had a negative impact on you?

- What are your feelings about sexual intimacy? What do you enjoy most about such intimacy? least? Are there any sexual acts that you don't want to do? Have you talked about what you like and don't like?

- What do you really want and need from your partner? (Include the whole range of sexual intimacy.)

- What are twenty things your partner does that count as "strokes" for you?

- What worries you about sex in your marriage? What do you look forward to?

- When, where, and how often do you anticipate having sex six months after you're married? How do you think your sexual relationship will change once you are married? What do you think it will be like in ten years? How do you feel about those changes?

- Has each of you been tested for HIV/AIDS and other sexually transmitted diseases? If not, do you plan to do so? (Testing for STDs is required in some states and provinces.) Have you discussed this with each other? Is there anything about your past experience you want to discuss before your wedding?

- What did you learn from this chapter? What decisions do you choose to make in response to what you learned?

℘ Marriage Enrichment

- What events or attitudes from your family of origin or your past experience have influenced your sexual behaviors and feelings? How have you dealt with those experiences or attitudes that have had a negative impact on you?

- What are your feelings about sexual intimacy? Is your current sexual relationship satisfying? What would you like to change?

- What do you enjoy most about sex? least? Are there any sexual acts that you are now doing that you don't want to do? Is there something you would like to do? Do you talk about what you like and don't like?

- What do you really want and need from your partner? (Include the whole range of sexual intimacy.)

- What are twenty things your partner does that count as "strokes" for you?

- What worries you about sex in your marriage?

- Before your wedding were each of you tested for HIV/AIDS and other sexually transmitted diseases? If not, do you plan to do so now? Have you discussed this with each other?

- How has your sexual relationship changed since your wedding? How do you feel about those changes? What do you think your sexual relationship will be like in ten years?

- What did you learn from this chapter? What decisions do you choose to make in response to what you learned?

QUESTIONS FOR GROUPS TO DISCUSS

- What messages did you get about sex from your family? school friends? church? culture? How do you think those messages affect your feelings about sex?

- What is your understanding of the role of sex in marriage?

- What is the difference between sexual activity and sexual intimacy?

- How might a couple better communicate about sex? When and where are good and not so good times to talk about your sex life?

- How did you react to the 20:1 ratio and saying "I love you" five times a day? Is there any pattern to how different people in the group react to those suggestions (age, gender, race)? Why might people react differently to those suggestions?

- What would you identify as abusive sexual behaviors? Do you see any patterns in how different people in your group identify what is or is not abusive?

- What would you identify as sexual misconduct on the part of a counselor, other professional (doctor, teacher), or member of your congregation or community? What would you do if you felt someone's behavior was inappropriate?

- Do you think a couple needs to discuss sexual matters such as rape, incest, abortion, AIDS, and STDs? Why or why not? What is the role of the community in these situations? What support would you want to give to couples in your congregation facing these issues?

- The prayer book says that "the union of husband and wife in heart, body, and mind is intended by God for their mutual joy...for the help and comfort they give one another...for the procreation of children." What is your understanding of the purpose of sex? How can sex be sacred?

- What did you learn from this chapter? What decisions do you choose to make in response to what you learned that you would like to share with others?

SUGGESTED PROJECTS

- Visit a bookstore and peruse the section that has books about sex. Buy a book or video that will give you some creative sexual ideas. Read or watch it together and discuss what appeals to you and what doesn't appeal to you.

- Many people are surprised to find that there is a passionate love poem in the Bible. Read the Song of Solomon together and discuss what you find. What do you think it is about? Why do you think those who established the canon of Christian scripture included this poem? What does it have to say to us about God, love, and sex?

The Gift of Children

Bestow on them, if it is your will, the gift and heritage of children, and
the grace to bring them up to know you, to love you, and to serve you.
(BCP 429)

The decisions facing a couple about children used to be quite simple: when will we have them and how many? A few couples may have decided not to have children or to adopt a child on principle rather than out of necessity, but, on the whole, couples assumed children were a part of what it meant to be married. Today for many couples the issues are far more complex. Many couples who are preparing for marriage already have children, either their own or from previous marriages. If for some reason couples are unable to have a child, there are now a host of options beyond adoption available to them, from artificial insemination to surrogate parenting. More couples are choosing not to have children, a decision that can be lived out in numerous ways—conscious and unconscious. Even the process of raising children has become more complex. For all of these reasons, it is important to discuss the place of children in your lives before you make them part of your relationship, and then to revisit that conversation frequently during your marriage.

The church affirms the belief that children are a gift from God. In addition to the biological drive to birth children merely for the propagation of the species, many people who love each other choose to create a child of that love. For some it is a desire to have a part of themselves that continues beyond their own life. For others it is a desire to create life out of the love that bonds them so closely to each other. For still others, the birth of a child comes without a conscious choice to have a child, but rather as the result of the choice to be in relationship with each other.

If you do not already have children, we suggest you wait until after you've been married at least two years. The first year of marriage is a stressful time because enormous adjustments have to occur in your lives. Bringing a child into your life together requires even more adjustment. A child will change the nature of your marriage and put heavy demands on each of you and your relationship. If possible, give yourself a couple of years to work through the adjustments, stabilize your relationship, and enjoy the time together. This is valuable bonding time that will strengthen your relationship and make the inclusion of a child easier. During that time, you can begin to discuss some of the following questions and issues and develop a common sense of if, when, and how you want to proceed.

Unplanned children usually are as much a joy as those we for whom plan. Unwanted children generally are the result of irresponsible action on the part of adults who have a wide range of birth control options available to them. Today we have more opportunities than ever before to make conscious choices in planning for children. We encourage you to make those choices thoughtfully and avoid accidentally having a child before you are ready, or finding yourself past the age to have a child and regretting it.

℘ To Have or Not to Have

Obviously, the first choice is whether you want children to be a part of your marriage relationship. We want to begin by saying that we believe that all of us, married or single, parent or childless adult, have a responsibility for the care and nurture of children. Children are a common responsibility of society and especially of the Christian community. Protecting, nurturing, guiding, and instructing the next generation is the responsibility of *all* adults. For this reason, we feel that the choice facing you is not *if* children will be part of your marriage but *how*.

This does not mean, however, that everyone needs to have or raise children full-time. Linda, for example, did not have children but chose to take time from parish ministry to serve as a foster parent for a child and mentor to that child's mother. Adults who do not have children can build close relationships with their nieces and nephews or children of friends and neighbors. They might be teachers in schools or church, youth leaders at camps or Y's, Big Brothers or Big Sisters. They might tutor children or coach Little League or counsel children. The possibilities are endless. Our point is that in some way those who choose not to have children still have a responsibility to care for and nurture children in whatever way is most appropriate for them.

Choosing to have and raise a child requires an enormous amount of time and energy, and can be very difficult. Some people do not have the personality, the physical or mental stamina, or the level of commitment required to do that. They may have other demands in their lives that preclude them from adequately carrying out the additional responsibilities of parenting. It is entirely appropriate for those couples to choose not to have or raise children.

If you choose not to have children, some people will label you as selfish, many will ask prying questions, and some may even try to shame you into having children. You can resist these attempts by others to lay their values or life perspectives on you by simply stating that you do not wish to discuss the subject. You may want to tell family members that you will not be having children once you have made and implemented a permanent decision (especially if the hints and questions are driving you nuts!). Remember, you do not owe anyone an explanation for your decision. This is a matter between the two of you. Simply state your decision and ask people to respect your wishes by not making it an ongoing topic of conversation.

ᛉ How to Have Children

What used to be a simple matter has the potential for becoming very complex in today's world of medicine! If you are fortunate enough to have made the choice, discontinued your birth control method, and conceived promptly, it still is simple. If, on the other hand, you experience difficulty conceiving a child, things are more complicated. Your options are much greater than they were even a few years ago; but along with those options are physical, emotional, and ethical complexities that also didn't exist before.

Couples unable to conceive a child of their own have always had the option of adopting a child. We want to hold up and affirm this decision, especially in the context of the Christian community. In the United States, Canada, and around the globe are countless children who face life alone, often in the bleakest circumstances. We can imagine no greater ministry than that of choosing to parent such a child. While many people have a strong desire to have a biological child, a number are will-

---

Adoption

In the service of Thanksgiving for the Adoption of a Child, the celebrant gives the child to the parents, saying:

As God has made us his children by adoption and grace, may you receive N. as your own son [daughter].

How is the adoption of a child symbolic of God's adoption of us?

ing and able to set aside those desires to give the gift of love to a child who might otherwise grow up alone and unloved.

If you are unable to have a biological child or if you can have children but choose to adopt, we encourage you to discuss adoption with your clergyperson, other adoptive parents, and adoption agencies. If adoption agencies are unable to assist you (perhaps because of their age restrictions) you may be able to arrange a private adoption. Try to avoid looking for the "perfect child"—that is, an infant that looks just like you and has no problems. Rather, look for the child God is calling you to parent.

If you have considered adoption and feel it is not for you, you may want to explore artificial insemination or other medical interventions to help you have a child. These medical advances can often work wonders and, when they do, they can help you conceive and birth a child. However, they are usually quite expensive and can be very draining physically and emotionally. If you choose this route, make sure you have the ongoing support you need. Discuss what is happening with your clergyperson,

---

In Vitro Fertilization

In vitro fertilization uses the male parent's sperm to impregnate the female parent's ovum in a petri dish in the laboratory. Those ova that are fertilized are then implanted in the womb.

This procedure gives hope to many childless couples but also raises ethical questions. Sometimes more ova are fertilized than are needed or desired. What happens to the others? Are they disposed of or used in other women? Some people question whether it is right to spend enormous sums of money to obtain a birth child while orphans go without adequate parenting. Others wonder if the cost restricts it to the wealthy or encourages poor women to "sell" their ova. Is this like selling a child?

Still others raise questions about the multiple births that often result—is it right to artificially generate five or six children whose low birth weights often place a severe financial burden on the medical system and parents? When resources are limited, does this mean that some couples have many children while the children of other couples die because funds are lacking to provide the necessary care?

More and more we need to learn how to balance our personal needs with the needs of others. Individual decisions have an impact on the broader community, so what you decide about these matters needs to be thoroughly discussed with each other and with others. Your clergyperson and other members of your congregation can help you think through these issues.

marriage mentor, family members, or friends who can listen, share your pain and uncertainty, and support you in love and prayer.

Finally, consider the practical and ethical issues that are presented by some of these options. Will your child know he or she was adopted, conceived through artificial insemination, or birthed by a surrogate parent? Will he or she have access to his or her biological parent(s) or information about them? What will you do if a surrogate parent refuses to part with the child after birth, or the birth parent wants the child back? What relationship, if any, will you have with the biological parents of your child? How much money should you spend in your attempt to have a child? Is it ethical to pay someone to be a surrogate parent? Is using a volunteer surrogate parent (for example, a sibling, your parent, a friend) ethical? What are the implications of these various birth options for you, your child, and your marriage?

These are not easy matters to sort through or decide. We strongly encourage you to discuss them with your clergyperson and/or counselor. Be aware of the need to make rational choices based on the best information you can get. But also be aware of the need to pray, to seek and follow God's leading. God's ability to create love and life out of the most painful and difficult situations is quite amazing. If you can stop and listen, God may lead you in directions you would never have imagined.

🙰 Maintaining Balance

When a marriage is new, it is normal for you to focus on your love relationship. When children are immediately present, they and their needs demand your attention. In the chaos of adjusting to a new life, it is easy to lose the balance and to focus too much either on your relationship as a couple or on your children. Either extreme is almost sure to cause problems. You must make your relationship a priority or you will be drained empty, unable to be effective parents. Waiting a couple of years before having children will give you time to strengthen the relationship for the stresses created by a new baby. If you don't have that luxury, you need to be even more careful to plan time alone together.

If you are into the first few years of marriage and already have one or two children, it may be time to check that balance. The demands of young children, especially if they come at the same time that job demands are also high, can drain a marriage. No matter how busy or how poor you are, you must set aside time and money to do things together without anyone else around. If you do not nurture your relationship, it will suffer, and the negative impact on your job and especially on your children will be high. Take some time and money from jobs and children and spend it on the relationship now. You will find it an investment that earns good interest later!

Whether you have children naturally, by adoption, or through the use of some medical means, you may also be faced with difficult problems. Your child may be born with some physical or neurological difficulties. Or, your child may become seriously ill or injured. You may have to make life-and-death decisions about what kind of medical care to provide or whether you should discontinue life support. A child with a genetic condition or a problem caused by the actions of the birth mother may result in feelings of guilt, shame, or blame. How will you deal with any of these situations? Who will support you? It is important for you to develop and maintain supportive relationships with friends, clergy, and family now who can help you through any difficult times you might encounter.

∞ When You Already Have Children

Many couples enter a marriage with one or more children from a previous marriage or relationship or as single adults who have had or adopted children. One of the first issues to be addressed in your marriage is how to incorporate these children into your new family. It is important to discuss as a couple how your marriage will affect the children. The decision to marry means that both of you now have responsibility for each child. Obviously the step-parent does not replace the child's birth parent, but he or she does have a relationship with the children, even if they are grown.

If your marriage will make you a step-parent and you are unfamiliar with the dynamics, it would be helpful to learn from others by talking with people in a similar situation, by reading books, and by attending workshops on blended family dynamics. Being accepted as a step-parent generally takes time—often it takes a *great deal* of time—and patience. You may find that you need to be calm and positive for years while your step-child ignores you or actively demonstrates dislike. Do not go into the marriage with the illusion that your step-child will come to love you soon, if ever. You can expect mutual respect; if something deeper than that develops, that's great (and often it does).

Step-parents often hope for more than a child can realistically give. Step-parenting often requires even more patience than parenting, as step-parents get much of the same pain and grief that children can create and few of the joys. Step-children, especially older children, rarely acknowledge positive feelings about step-parents, even when they have them: to express love or affection toward a step-parent may make them feel they are being disloyal to their birth parent. As a step-parent your job is to be mature enough to recognize these dynamics and to be a steady, reliable adult who cares about them. Over time, that may develop into a positive and rewarding relationship for both of you.

While step-parents may or may not gain the rewards of having a child, they do acquire the responsibilities. When you marry, your partner brings "all that I am and all that I have"—and that includes children. When you accept your partner, you accept his or her children and you accept responsibility for them. You may not be the primary caregiver, but some of your joint income, time, and energy will go toward raising them. Even if they are adults or young adults, you have a responsibility to work with your partner to plan for their inheritance and respond to their needs. If the two of you have a child of your own, it may be tempting to put your step-children in second place, but doing so will be destructive of your partner's relationship with his or her children and of your relationship with each other.

When bringing a new adult into a family, parents need to pay special attention to their children, whether they live with you or will be with you part-time. Your children probably did not have a real choice about this marriage. They may not know your new partner well or be especially comfortable with—much less like—him or her. Even if they know and like your partner, the wedding and transition time creates confusing feelings for a child of any age. Children, almost without exception, want their parents to be together and to live happily ever after. The fact that your previous relationship was turbulent or abusive or that the child's other parent was absent or died often doesn't matter. Many children still hold onto that dream, even into their adult years. They may seem pleased with your wedding, yet underneath children generally have

---

Child Abuse

Every adult has a responsibility to protect any child from physical, sexual, or emotional abuse. If you or your partner hit a child in anger, are verbally abusive, or become sexually involved with a child in any way, seek help immediately. If either of you suffered abuse as a child, you are at risk for abusing your child. If you see warning signs in your behavior, seek professional help to develop appropriate parenting skills. Your clergyperson can help you identify where to find help in your community. Take action as soon as you feel that "something is not right." It is better to intervene early and get help than to let it go to the point where a child is seriously hurt.

It is important to be aware that there are people who abuse children. They can be trusted members of your family or community, as well as strangers. In the past these incidents were often hidden, ignored, or even accepted. Today we recognize the responsibility we all have to protect children. If you feel any child is being abused, seek help. In case of an emergency, most community phonebooks list a child abuse agency or hotline number, or you can call the police any time, day or night.

mixed feelings. Plus, they have to face living in a new household or coming into a new living situation for weekends or holiday visits.

It is important to recognize these feelings and help children of all ages to adjust. Time (often counted in years), acceptance of their feelings, and honest conversation about them generally resolves the difficulties. There are self-help books that can give you information about discipline, communication, and other issues you may encounter. If you have difficulties, it is often wise to see a counselor before the problems become embedded or undermine your relationship.

One other issue you may want to consider: many couples choose to adopt their partner's child, especially if the child is young and the birth parent has died or has no interest in parenting the child. Obviously, this would not be appropriate if the birth parent is actively involved in raising the child. However, if the birth parent is absent, adopting can be a way to help a child feel accepted and secure. It also guarantees guardianship in case the child's remaining parent also dies. Take care not to force this option on a child, however. Allow time for relationships to develop and for the child to express a desire for adoption.

& Raising Children

Once you have decided to have children (or if you already have them), the next issues to emerge are differences in how to raise them. Again, it is useful to understand each other's personal history, since we learn how to parent from our own experiences of being parented. If significant differences in expectations concerning discipline, habits, lifestyle, or behavior emerge, discuss them thoroughly and frequently.

Two of the most important elements in raising children are that the two of you agree on what you will do and that you are consistent. A child with two parents sending opposite and inconsistent messages about expectations, behavior, and lifestyle will be very confused. A child with two loving parents who establish and maintain consistent messages will generally be fine. Lots of tender, loving care, along with a healthy dose of common sense and lots of courage and fortitude, will help you get through most of the ups and downs of child rearing.

We began this chapter by acknowledging that children are a gift from God. While the immediate parents play the primary role for the care and nurture of children, the entire community, especially those of us who are a part of a Christian community, are responsible for the upbringing of the children entrusted to our care. We encourage you to give serious consideration to how you will form your child in the Christian faith. The wedding service asks God to give you the grace to bring them up to know, love, and serve God (BCP 429). Dropping your children off at church school on Sunday mornings or just taking them to church with you is not likely to do that job. We believe that the best way you can help your child come to know God is to speak freely and openly about your own faith life, to have some regular prayer in your home (grace at meals, devotions, bedtime prayers), and to demonstrate clearly your love for each other and your service to others.

Children learn by observing and doing. If you live a faithful Christian life some of that will rub off—even though it might not look like it when they're teenagers! Be patient. Your life and witness during their childhood may not bear fruit until they are older and have their own children, or have experiences that cause them to turn to their faith foundation. Your job is not to make your child's faith decisions; your job is to live as a faithful Christian and bear witness to the faith that is in you. Your child will make his or her own decisions in due time.

∾   A Lifelong Commitment

Choosing to have a child makes that human being a part of your lifelong commitment to each other. Even if your marriage ends or one partner dies, you will always be that child's parent and therefore you will always be connected, in some way, to that child's other parent. The three of you are forever bound together. Parenting is a lifelong, life-altering commitment. Other joint decisions a couple may make—the choice of where and how to live, even whether to remain married—can be reversed if not undone. But the decision to have or adopt children, once made, is a lifelong commitment.

Interfaith Marriages

Raising children within interfaith marriages presents a particular opportunity and responsibility. Some parents expose children to both faiths and encourage them to choose the one most compelling to them. This option requires considerable investment of time and energy by both parents, as well as great sensitivity. Care must be taken to avoid putting a child in the position of having to choose for or against one parent.

We have seen couples successfully raise their children in one faith while exposing them to another. This places the choice in the hands of the adults, who are responsible for creating the dual faith situation. Children raised in this manner will be exposed to both faiths and so could choose to switch when they become adults, but they do not grow up with the pressure of making that choice while too young to do so. In making these decisions, it is important to make the child's needs primary. Discussions with clergy and other professionals can help you plan how you will address this situation.

There are important lessons to be learned from parenting. Del is a doting parent who continues to be deeply devoted and connected to his two sons, even though they are now "maturing adults" who are physically bigger than he and living on their own. As children grow and move from dependence on adults to independence, parents learn through their children's growth experiences the important virtues of vulnerability and humility. Parents share deeply all of their child's joys and sorrows.

O God, you have taught us through your blessed Son that whoever receives a little child in the name of Christ receives Christ himself: We give you thanks for the blessing you have bestowed on this family in giving them a child. Confirm their joy by a lively sense of your presence with them, and give them calm strength and patient wisdom as they seek to bring this child to love all that is true and noble, just and pure, lovable and gracious, excellent and admirable, following the example of our Lord and Saviour, Jesus Christ. Amen. (BCP 443)

With the passing of time and as the life-cycle continues, the parenting roles reverse themselves. Children become parents to their own children and, in many cases, caregivers to their parents. We come into the world dependent on God and our parents; we leave life dependent on God and our children. The transition from dependence to independence to interdependence and finally the return to dependence completes the cycle of life.

QUESTIONS FOR COUPLES
TO DISCUSS

‿ Marriage Preparation

- What was your experience of childhood? What did you especially like about your childhood that you would like for your children? What would you want to do differently?

- Are either of you adopted? Have you experienced a parent's divorce, the death of a parent, or a parent's remarriage? What was that like for you? How do you think those experiences may affect your marriage?

- Discuss your prior experience with children (siblings, babysitting, parenting).

- Do you want to have any children? If so, how many and when? If not, why not? Are you in agreement on this? If not, how will you handle your differences?

- What birth control method are you/will you use? Who is responsible for it?

- What would you do if you could not have children biologically? How do you feel about adoption? artificial insemination? abortion? other medical interventions? Do the two of you agree?

- What impact do you think having children will have on your careers and lifestyle?

- What are your expectations about caregiving roles? discipline styles? lifestyle (formal/informal, structured/unstructured)? What are your expectations for your children (appearance, talent, intelligence)?

- How do you think you would handle parenting a child who was disabled? a mediocre student? a rebellious adolescent? How do you think you would live with the death of a child?

- Do either of you have children? If yes, what is each partner's relationship with those children? What is each partner's relationship with the children's birth parent? grandparents?

- If you have children, how do they feel about your partner? the marriage? How will they participate in the wedding and in establishing your new home together?

- If you will be a step-parent, talk about how you feel about that role and your expectations. If you are the birth parent, talk about the role of step-parent as you perceive it and your expectations. Where do you anticipate difficulties and how will the two of you handle them?

- Who would take custody of your children if you divorced or both died?

- How would you raise your children to know, love, and serve God?

- What have you learned from this chapter? What decisions do you choose to make in response to what you learned?

◐ Marriage Enrichment

- What was your experience of childhood? What did you especially like about your childhood that you would like for your children? What would you want to do differently?

- Are either of you adopted? Have you experienced a parent's divorce, the death of a parent, or a parent's remarriage? What was that like for you? How do you think those experiences have affected your marriage?

- Discuss your experience with children (siblings, babysitting, parenting).

- If you do not already have children, do you want to have them? If so, how many and when? If not, why not? Are you in agreement on this? If not, how will you handle your differences?

- What birth control method are you using? Who is responsible for it?

- What would you do if you could not have children biologically? How do you feel about adoption? artificial insemination? abortion? other medical interventions? Do the two of you agree?

- What impact do you think having children has had (or will have) on your careers and lifestyle?

- What are your expectations about caregiving roles? discipline styles? lifestyle (formal/informal, structured/unstructured)? What are your expectations for your children (appearance, talent, intelligence)?

- How do you think you would handle parenting a child who was disabled? a mediocre student? a rebellious adolescent? How do you think you would live with the death of a child?

- Did either of you have children from a previous relationship? If yes, what is each spouse's relationship with those children? What is each spouse's relationship with the children's birth parent? grandparents?

- If you are a step-parent, talk about how you feel about that role and your expectations. If you are the birth-parent, talk about the role of the step-parent as you perceive it and your expectations. Where have you encountered difficulties and how did the two of you handle them? Where might you go for help?

- Who would take custody of your children if you divorced or both died?

- How do you raise your children to know, love, and serve God?

- What have you learned from this chapter? What decisions do you choose to make in response to what you learned?

QUESTIONS FOR GROUPS
TO DISCUSS

- What did you especially like about your childhood that you would like for your children? What would you want to do differently?

- Are any of you adopted? Have you experienced a parent's divorce, the death of a parent, or a parent's remarriage? What was that like for you? How do you think those experiences may affect your marriage?

- What prior experience do you have with children (siblings, babysitting, parenting)?

- Why might a couple decide not to have children? Why might a couple decide to wait? What might be the consequences of those decisions? What might be the consequences of having children too quickly or without planning?

- What impact do you think having children has on careers and lifestyles?

- What are your expectations about caregiving roles? discipline styles? lifestyle? What are your expectations for your children (appearance, talent, intelligence)?

- How do you think you would handle parenting a child who was disabled? a mediocre student? a rebellious adolescent? How do you think you would live with the death of a child?

- How do you feel about adoption? artificial insemination? abortion? other medical interventions?

- Have you made plans for who would take custody of your children if you divorced or both died?

- How would you raise your children to know, love, and serve God?

- What are the three most important things you want for your children?

- What have you learned from this chapter and discussion? What decisions do you choose to make in response to what you learned?

SUGGESTED   PROJECTS

- *If you are not parents:* "Borrow" a child for a day or two. If possible, take care of one younger child and an older child. Then talk about your feelings, the roles each of you assumed, and how you worked together.

- *If you are parents:* Plan a day or two away from your children. Talk about the impact having children has had on you and your marriage, and what you especially value about having children.

NINE

Yes, No, Maybe, Why Bother?

I. MARRIAGE PREPARATION

Therefore, marriage is not to be entered into unadvisedly or lightly, but reverently,
deliberately, and in accordance with the purposes for which it was instituted by God.
(BCP 423)

Note: If you are already married, skip this section and move on to the second half of
this chapter on Marriage Enrichment.

If you've read this far, the chances are highly likely that you are settled in your plans to get married. Nevertheless, now is the time for the two of you to sit down and really decide if that is what you want to do and if this is when you want to do it. As the prayer book says, "Marriage is not to be entered into unadvisedly or lightly, but reverently, deliberately, and in accordance with the purposes for which it was instituted by God." Your discussion of the previous chapters has probably created one of four responses in you: a heartfelt affirmation of your decision to marry, a sinking feeling that you really don't want to get married, an increasing confusion and anxiety about whether this is really what you want to do, or a stronger sense of "why bother getting married at all?" This section of the book is here to help you look directly at the questions, "Do I really want to get married? Am I ready and willing to make that commitment?" and we will suggest some ways you might handle varying responses to them.

∾ Yes!

You've read and thought about the issues we have raised. The two of you have discussed things and worked through any difficulties that emerged. You feel confident about your decision to proceed (although perhaps with a few butterflies!). Now, what are you really deciding to do?

You are making a lifelong commitment to live in a loving relationship with your partner. You are choosing this person as the one you will love, trust, and treasure above all others. You are choosing this person to become one with you in heart and soul. You are deciding that this relationship is where you will offer yourself to be "a sign of Christ's love to this sinful and broken world" (BCP 429). You are deciding that in this relationship you will ask God's will and spirit to become one with yours, thus binding you to God and to each other. You are deciding that here is where you will live, learn, and grow in the mystery of love.

This decision requires love and commitment. You must love your partner now and be committed to doing what is necessary to continue in a loving relationship five, ten, fifty years from now. Such a commitment means being willing and able to make the inevitable sacrifices needed for your love to grow deeper and stronger. It means being willing and able to "hang in there" through thick and thin, in good times and bad, when you're happy and when you're unhappy, when you feel love and when you don't.

Marriage means choosing to travel on a journey together. You will have to travel anyway—all of us move through the ups and downs of life. Choosing to marry means choosing to go through those ups and downs together—loving, challenging, supporting, and encouraging each other as you go. The journey through life is different when you're together rather than traveling alone. Like any choice, there are costs and there are benefits in choosing to marry. Those of us who choose to marry weigh the costs and accept them to gain the benefits that come with traveling through life with the one we love.

If this is where you are, say "yes" with all your heart, your mind, and your soul. Make this choice wholeheartedly. Throw yourself into this relationship with abandon. Seek God's blessing and the church's blessing. And know that wherever the road takes you, God's loving presence is with you, always ready to renew and rekindle love in each of you, love that makes us new creatures in God every day.

∾ No!

You've just read the paragraphs above and know this is not where you are. Each chapter you read made it clearer that there were far too many problems, or that your heart just wasn't in it. The discussions with your partner were conflicted or painful or they were just surface chit-chat to avoid really talking about the issues. You realize that getting married, at least right now and to this person, is not what you want. Now what do you do?

Announcements may have been made. Invitations may have been sent. Deposits and purchases may have already been completed. Your partner may be committed to proceed. How can you face the embarrassment, loss of money, and pain that turning back would create?

First, recognize that the temporary embarrassment and loss of money are insignificant in comparison to the enormous difficulties created by proceeding with a marriage you don't want. Even your partner's pain at cancelling a wedding now is minor in comparison to the pain that will come later at the discovery that your commitment never existed in the first place. If you cannot wholeheartedly say "yes," you need to say "no."

Explaining a "No" Decision to Others

You've decided not to proceed with the wedding. How do you handle telling your family and friends? If you want to handle it quickly, a written note would be appropriate (especially so if invitations have been sent) or you can tell them individually (by phone or in person). Family members and attendants should be told personally. You do not need to explain why; simply state that the two of you have decided not to proceed. If you want to soften it you can add "at this time," but recognize that people will then keep asking you if you've rescheduled the wedding.

Above all, remember that you don't owe anyone an explanation. Do not allow anyone to pry into your business. If someone asks, tell them, "I don't care to discuss that." Period. If they persist, you can ask them, "Why are you asking me to talk about something I've said I don't care to discuss?" This gets the focus off you and onto their inappropriate behavior.

If you have made the decision for yourself and must tell your partner, do so as promptly, kindly, and gently as possible. Be as supportive as you can, but understand that when you have broken someone's heart, you cannot fix it. It must mend in its own way and in its own time. If you have decided to end the relationship, then end it cleanly so you and your partner can both get on with your lives. Give yourself time and space to grieve the loss of the relationship and your hopes and dreams for it.

In all of these cases you may wish to talk with your clergyperson about how to proceed and to seek his or her support during this painful time.

Trust your instincts. If your reading and discussions have made you uneasy or uncomfortable about something, don't just ignore it and proceed. At least stop and investigate your thoughts and feelings with your clergyperson or a counselor; then decide what to do.

Red Flags

It may be helpful for us to share our opinion about times we believe one should not get married. We will also raise some situations which we believe indicate a need for seriously rethinking the decision to marry. If you find yourself in any of the following situations, we strongly urge you to seek help from your clergyperson or a counselor immediately.

One of the most important red flags is abuse or addiction. If your partner is abusive (physically, mentally, or sexually) or an active addict, do not get married. Abuse and addiction must be addressed promptly and thoroughly before there is any hope of establishing a healthy marriage. Your partner will probably protest when you decide not to proceed; he or she will probably promise not to do it again, claim he or she is "better" or declare "I can't live without you." Ignore these promises and pleas—they are part of the illness. You are not responsible for your partner's behavior or happiness. Nor can you fix your partner or make him or her choose to deal with the problem. Your partner needs to make those choices.

If your partner has been an addict or abusive in the past, do not assume that all is well. The illness may simply be "in remission," so to speak. An addict or abuser needs to stop the behavior for a significant period of time (count years, not weeks), receive therapy to address the underlying psychological problems, and be committed to a lifelong process of recovery. If you choose to marry someone with a history of addiction or abuse, please talk with your clergyperson or a counselor first. Understand that you join your spouse in a lifetime of dealing with that illness. You need to plan how you will address problems if and when they occur (identify service agencies, save money to pay for counseling, and so on) in the same way you would plan for any other lifelong disease.

If you *suspect* your partner is an addict or abusive but aren't sure, talk with a counselor trained in this area of work. Go by yourself first and describe what makes you wonder. Ask the counselor to help you assess whether you are in an addictive or abusive relationship. And remember, trust your instincts.

Second, you need seriously to consider saying "no" to marriage if you are unsure and are feeling pressured. Maybe things don't seem to "add up"; there are gaps in your partner's history or something about your partner that just doesn't feel right. Be especially cautious if you are having these feelings and you have something your partner really desires (house, money, children) and/or you just met your partner a few weeks or months ago. While we know that many brief courtships result in good marriages, it is generally better to know your partner for a good period of time. (Linda's personal rule was two years; she assumed by then she had seen and learned enough to know what she was getting into.) In any case, it is this combination of haste, pressure, and uneasiness that suggests the need for a halt in the proceedings at this point.

Another red flag is when one or both of you go into the marriage with an attitude of "If it doesn't work out we can always get divorced." This attitude tends to become a self-fulfilling prophecy. It signals a lack of complete commitment and creates an environment that undermines the marital relationship. We have both learned—in the school of hard knocks—that divorce is extremely painful, disruptive, and destructive. It takes literally years to recover from a divorce (if you ever do) and many innocent bystanders are hurt along the way. Do not go into a marriage if you intend to get divorced. If your partner has this attitude, we encourage you to reconsider the marriage. The chances are quite likely that he or she will pull out even if you yourself are committed.

If you or your partner have been through multiple marriages and divorces in the past, it is even more important that you take your time in making this decision, seek counseling, and make sure that you are committed to the relationship, to the marriage, *and* to doing the work necessary to make it work. The best test of that is to establish good habits of working together, good communication, and good use of resources (counselors, for example) *before* the wedding. If you can't do it now, it is doubtful you will do it after the wedding. Remember, marriage is a process, so there is no good excuse for putting off what needs to be done. Start now and when you have convinced yourself, your partner, and those working with you that you are committed and have developed appropriate skills, *then* plan on getting married.

∾ **Maybe**

You're indecisive. You found the readings and discussions helpful. Some things felt really good; some were a problem. Maybe there's one thing that keeps "bugging" you. Or something in your past or present that you haven't quite resolved. Or one of you is much more enthused about and committed to the relationship than the other. Whatever it is, you are now wondering whether you should proceed.

The first decision you may want to make is "not yet" to give yourself time to address whatever is holding you back. If you can identify the problem or the issue, spend some time working on it with your clergyperson or a counselor. You will want to make some significant progress, but you don't necessarily have to "fix" everything before you get married! Pay as much attention to *how* you and your partner work on the problem as you do to resolving the issue itself. If you have good communication, high energy, strong commitment, and are working on the issue *productively*, you probably will be able to work it through during your marriage. If working on that issue creates problems in your relationship or produces no visible progress, you may want to say "no" to the marriage or at least wait until you've given it more time.

If there is a major imbalance in commitment, you need to address that imbalance before you proceed. There are two ways to go at that. Sometimes one partner has a "fear of commitment" that may be resolved in discussions with a clergyperson or counselor. Or it may require the high commitment partner to lower his or her commitment or even withdraw it. We often make unconscious emotional contracts with each other ("You take care of this emotional need in our relationship and I'll take care of that need"). If one partner's commitment level is very high, he or she may be carrying the commitment load for the two of you. You may discover that the low commitment partner's commitment level comes up when the high commitment partner lowers or withdraws his or her commitment. This is a rather complicated psychological dance that you may want to discuss with a counselor.

Finally, if your decision is not wholeheartedly "yes" but not clearly "no" either, give yourself time. This is an important decision and there is no real reason why you need to make it while you are uncertain. Do what you need to do to understand and resolve your uncertainty. But don't let yourself get pressured into doing something you aren't committed to.

& Why Bother?

You're engaged because your partner wants to get married, or your parents want you to get married, or because you think maybe you "ought to" get married. But you really don't know whether getting married is worth the bother. You've read the book, participated in the discussions, and decided that it really looks like more trouble than it's worth. After all, the current divorce rate is about fifty percent anyway. So why bother getting married? Why not just live together for as long as it works?

This is a serious question. Today, more than ever, couples are choosing to live together without getting married. Some do so because of their experience of other people's divorces and a subsequent disillusionment about the institution of marriage. Others have a general distrust of institutions—a disposition that is pervasive in our culture today. Still others find that changing gender roles, changing jobs, changing technologies, changing everything has made life seem unstable and lifelong commitments too risky. In such a culture the "Why bother?" question arises naturally. We would like to address this question from several perspectives—practical, emotional, and spiritual.

First, choosing to love someone and to live with them for a period of time means that you are already on the marriage journey. Marriage is a process, not an event. The wedding itself is a public acknowledgement and celebration of the marriage the couple has already begun, a time when the couple seeks the blessing of God and the church on their marriage as it then exists and as it goes forward.

"Just living together" avoids that public commitment, but it does not protect you from the impact of being married. This is why most states legally recognize a couple who has lived together "as man and wife" for a certain period of time (perhaps five years) as married. It's called a common law marriage: your actions created the legal marriage even though you did not sign a marriage license or say any marriage vows. Practically speaking, if you live as if you're married, you receive the rights and take on the responsibilities of the marriage contract. In other words, if it looks like a duck, walks like a duck, and quacks like a duck, it's probably a duck!

Just living together does not protect you from the emotional pain of divorce, either. When you love someone and share your life with them for years, leaving that relationship will be just as painful as leaving a spouse. Any children you might have will be just as devastated as they would if you were getting a legal divorce. Your friends and family will be emotionally affected in much the same way as they would if you were married. The tangled web of love grows whether it has a marriage license or not. You delude yourself if you think that you can love and leave without feeling or causing pain as long as you don't get married. Loving and leaving always hurts.

The spiritual benefits of getting married, rather than just living together, are greater than most of us realize. In marriage we make our commitment to one another before God and the church, and we seek the blessing of each. Most people assume that the blessing does some good (or at least does no harm!). Many people recognize that making a public commitment strengthens one's inner resolve to keep that commitment. But there is more to the spiritual side of marriage than that.

Marriage is a sacrament. That means it is a *sign* and a *symbol*. It is a *sign* of the unity of Christ and the church. The dictionary tells us that a sign "suggests the presence or existence of a fact, condition or quality not immediately evident." A Christian marriage suggests the presence of a loving relationship between Christ and the body of Christ. Beyond that, marriage is a *symbol*. A symbol points to a reality and simultaneously participates in that reality. Marriage is a symbol in that it points to and becomes a part of Christ's relationship with the people of God, while Christ's relationship with the people of God becomes part of a marriage.

That rather complex theology might be stated more simply: in marriage, we encounter Christ in a way we do not encounter Christ anywhere else. Obviously, marriage is not the only place we encounter Christ, but in the marriage relationship we do so in a way that is different from how we encounter Christ in worship, in parental love, in nature, or in other parts of our lives. A key (although not only) aspect of what makes the marriage encounter different is that we have made a public, lifelong commitment of unconditional love, just as Christ's life, death, resurrection, and promise to be with us always (Matt. 28:20) is a public, eternity-long commitment of unconditional love. Our commitment in marriage is only a small sign of that great love. And yet our marriage becomes a powerful symbol to us and to the world because we bear witness to Christ's love, and Christ's presence in our lives becomes love in our midst.

Getting married makes a difference. Not that God loves you any more or less. Getting married makes a difference because it creates an opportunity for you to experience Christ's love in that relationship and it creates an opportunity for that relationship to "show forth" Christ's love to others.

Note: Skip the next section for those who are already married,
and move on to the questions at the end of the chapter.

II. MARRIAGE ENRICHMENT

Grant that all married persons who have witnessed these vows may find
their lives strengthened and their loyalties confirmed.
(BCP 430)

You and your spouse have read the material thus far and now have an opportunity to reflect on your marriage and your decision to marry. "Wait a minute," you say, "we already made that decision!" It is true that you made the decision to have a wedding and make your commitment to each other public. But it is also true that we make the decision to be married each and every day. A relationship is either growing or dying. Every day we have an opportunity to choose to love and to do and be what will help our marriage grow. Choosing to neglect the relationship or to do and be what damages it causes our marriage to die. So the choice is a daily choice. Most of us make that daily choice unconsciously. We now invite you to reflect on your choice and make it consciously.

ᔥ Yes!

You've read and thought about the issues we have raised. The two of you discussed things and worked through any difficulties that emerged. You feel comfortable with your marriage and confident about reaffirming your lifelong commitment to live in a loving relationship with your partner. This is, in fact, the person you choose as the one person whom you love, trust, and treasure above all others; you are becoming one in heart and soul. In this relationship you have and will continue to offer yourself to be "a sign of Christ's love to this sinful and broken world" (BCP 429). You want this relationship to be the place where you ask God's will and spirit to become one with yours, thus binding you to God and to each other. Here is where you choose to live and learn and grow in the mystery of love.

As you already know, this choice requires love and commitment. You must love your partner today and every day and you must be committed to doing what is necessary to continue in a loving relationship five, ten, or fifty years from now. Such a commitment means being willing and able to make the inevitable sacrifices needed for your love to grow deeper and stronger. It means being willing and able to "hang in there" through thick and thin, in good times and bad, when you're happy and when you're unhappy, when you feel love and when you don't.

And, as you already know, this choice is a wonderful gift of being loved, challenged, and supported as you travel the journey of life. Like any choice, there are costs and there are benefits in choosing to marry. You are more than willing to accept the costs because you have already gained many of the benefits that come with traveling through life with the one you love.

If this is where you are, say "yes" with all your heart, your mind, and your soul. Make this choice today and every day. On your wedding day you sought God's blessing and the church's blessing. Today, you know that wherever the road takes you, God's loving presence is with you, always ready to renew and strengthen the love in each of you that makes us new creatures in God every day.

ॐ No!

You have just read the paragraphs above and know that is not where you are. Each chapter you read made it clearer that there are a host of problems in your marriage or that your heart just isn't in it. The discussions with your spouse were conflicted or painful or they were just surface chit-chat to avoid really talking about the issues. You may feel fearful, depressed, or angry because deep in your heart you sense that your marriage is dead or dying. Now what do you do?

Trust your instincts. If your reading and discussions made you uneasy or uncomfortable about something, don't just ignore it and go on as usual. At least investigate those feelings with each other, a trusted friend, your clergyperson, and/or a counselor.

We want to discourage you from considering divorce as an immediate option, especially if you think it will be a solution to all your problems. We have both learned—in the school of hard knocks—that divorce is extremely painful, disruptive, and destructive. It literally takes years to recover from a divorce (if you ever do recover) and it hurts lots of innocent bystanders along the way. Often, in divorce you merely swap one set of problems for another. Before you choose divorce, put the effort into understanding what is wrong with this marriage and what is needed to renew and rebuild the love you once had. The attitude that says "If it doesn't work out we can always get divorced" tends to become a self-fulfilling prophecy. It creates an environment that undermines the marital relationship. Try a different self-fulfilling prophecy, an attitude that says "If we encounter problems, we will find a way to resolve them."

If you are thinking about divorce, or if you are considering going on "as is" while knowing that your relationship is dying, we urge you to seek help immediately. The sooner you begin to work on the problems in your marriage, the sooner you can begin to build a healthy, loving relationship. Putting it off until tomorrow rarely helps and usually hurts the relationship.

This is not a marital counseling book, nor can we cover all the issues that might be leading you to say "no" to your marriage. However, we can lay out a few simple realities. The first is that whatever your problem, it is almost certain that the way you and your spouse relate to each other creates or supports that problem. Before the problem can be resolved, something in your relationship needs to change.

Another basic reality is that you cannot change someone else; you can only change yourself. The changes you make *will* change the situation, which may resolve the problem or at least create new opportunities for its resolution. Usually we waste our energy hoping to resolve problems by getting our spouse to change. Focus on what

---

Addiction or Abuse in Marriage

Abuse and addiction must be addressed promptly and thoroughly before there is any hope of building a healthy marriage. It is often necessary for the healthier spouse to deliver an ultimatum: stop and get help or get out. If you do that, your spouse will probably promise not to do it again, claim to be "better," declare "I can't live without you." Ignore these promises and pleas—they are part of the abusive/addictive illness. You are not responsible for your spouse's behavior or happiness. Nor can you fix him or her, or make your spouse choose to deal with the problem. No one but your spouse can make those choices.

An addict or abuser needs to stop the behavior for a significant period of time (count years, not weeks), receive therapy to address the underlying psychological problems, and be committed to working on the illness for the rest of his or her life. If you are married to an addict or abuser, you have undoubtedly been an "enabler"—that is, you have most likely helped your spouse continue this behavior by not saying "no." If you want a healthy marriage, you must say "no."

Please talk with your priest or a counselor before you decide when, where, and how to say "no." While separation is often inevitable and divorce may be necessary, you and your spouse also may be able to work through these problems. Much of it will depend on the addict/abuser's willingness to face reality and deal with it. The important point is that you should not accept abusive behavior (and addicts are usually abusive in some fashion). If you have children, you have a special responsibility to make sure they are not subject to your spouse's abuse.

Finally, if you *suspect* your spouse is an addict or abusive but aren't sure, talk with a counselor trained in this area of work. Go by yourself first and describe what makes you wonder. Ask the counselor to help you assess whether you are in an addictive or abusive relationship.

you contribute to the problem, what *you* want or need, and what *you* are willing and able to do. Your spouse must take responsibility for himself or herself.

Although we urge you not to see divorce as an easy solution or as the only solution, there *are* a few situations in which divorce may be necessary. The primary one is if your spouse is abusive (physically, mentally, or sexually) or an addict who is unwilling to address the problem. But many marriages, and even some of these, are able to be healed.

Divorce often creates as many problems as it solves. And ultimately you will need to learn the painful lessons about yourself, make the necessary changes, and invest the time and energy into building a new relationship with someone else anyway. So you may as well invest it in what you have, if possible! Once you love someone deeply, you love them (in some way) forever. That spark of love may be small and weak, but it is still there and you can still rekindle it. Taking the time to learn the lessons and make the changes now can rebuild a love you once had and save you the pain of a divorce.

> ### Canon on the Dissolution of Marriage
>
> The Episcopal Church has several canons (regulations) about marriage. One of those is about divorce. It says:
>
> *When marital unity is imperiled by dissension, it shall be the duty of either or both parties, before contemplating legal action, to lay the matter before a Member of the Clergy; and it shall be the duty of such Member of the Clergy to labor that the parties may be reconciled.*
> (Constitution and Canons, 1991)
>
> While divorce is no longer forbidden, it is clear that members have a duty—an obligation—to seek the church's help whenever their marriage is in trouble. What would you do in such a case? To whom would bring your difficulties? What would you expect your clergyperson to do or say?

The amount of emotional effort needed to go through a divorce is tremendous. Investing some of the energy into working on what you have (or had) is a worthwhile investment. We live in an age where we assume that relationships are interchangeable or that we can fix relationships as quickly as we fix machines. This is not true. If you leave this relationship, there are good things in it that you can never regain. You may discover other good things elsewhere, but some things will be gone forever. While you can't *fix* a relationship, you can learn ways to live and grow in love if you are willing to invest the time and energy in doing so.

If the two of you find yourself divided on the question of divorce, with one person saying "let's get divorced" and the other saying "let's work on the marriage," we encourage you to choose to work on your marriage. We especially encourage the more positive spouse not to give up easily. If you love your spouse, this marriage is worth fighting for.

Finally, we urge you to talk with your clergyperson, even if you are seeing or plan to see a marriage counselor. Many counselors sincerely want to help you be happy; however, if they do not highly value the preservation of marriage, they may encourage you to see divorce as a way to achieve that happiness. In your pain and confusion you may respond to that encouragement and later regret it. Your clergyperson and your Christian community have a responsibility to hold you accountable for the vows you made before God *and* they have a responsibility to support you in prayer and in love. You may be surprised to discover what a difference the support of a loving Christian community can make in your marriage.

You may wonder why we, who have both been divorced, so strongly discourage divorce as a choice. While it is true that our second marriage has been a gift for which we are grateful, we are also aware of the enormous cost our divorces have brought to us and those we love. In retrospect, we are aware of how those to whom we turned for help encouraged us to divorce rather than to work through our problems. We and our spouses sought counseling (individually and jointly) and wanted our marriages to work. Both of us had marriages that were not beyond reclamation. But all of our counselors encouraged us to seek personal happiness by starting over, and our church advisors merely agreed that this might be the best route.

While we know there is always ample opportunity for establishing new relationships that are more satisfying, the reality is that lessons learned in new relationships often could have been learned in the original marriage if the couple and counselors were focused on restoring the marriage to wholeness. For this reason, we urge couples to seek this kind of help before divorcing. While some partners in a divorce may find life better for them afterwards, many of the other people involved will not. We have a responsibility for more than our individual happiness; we have a responsibility for the well-being of our families as well.

ᛒ Maybe

You're indecisive. You found the readings and discussions helpful. Some of them were reassuring; others set off a warning bell. Maybe there's one thing that keeps "bugging" you. Perhaps there is something in your past that you haven't quite resolved, or one of you is much more enthused about and committed to the relationship than the other. Whatever it is, you are now wondering whether you want to stay in the marriage or get divorced.

The first decision you may want to make is to give yourself time to address whatever is holding you back. If you can identify the problem or the issue, spend some time working on it with your clergyperson or a counselor, as discussed in the section above.

If there is a major imbalance in commitment, you need to address that imbalance. Sometimes one spouse has a problem that may be resolved in discussions with a clergyperson or counselor. Sometimes one spouse may simply say "no" to divorce and choose to do whatever is necessary to make the marriage work. Or sometimes it may require the highly committed spouse to back off a little. We often make unconscious emotional contracts with each other ("you take care of this emotional need in our relationship and I'll take care of that need"). If one spouse's commitment level is very high, he or she may be carrying the load for the two of you. You may discover that one spouse's commitment increases as the other decreases, a complex psychological dance that you need to discuss with a counselor.

Finally, if your decision is not wholeheartedly "yes" but not clearly "no" either, give yourself time and look for help in sorting out what might be causing the difficulty for you. Don't push yourself or let yourself get pressured into doing something hastily.

Why Bother?

The spiritual benefits of getting married, rather than just living together, are greater than most of us realize. In marriage we make our commitment to one another before God and the church, and we seek the blessing of each. Most people assume that the blessing does some good (or at least does no harm!). Many people recognize that making a public commitment strengthens one's inner resolve to keep that commitment. But there is more to the spiritual side of marriage than that.

Marriage is a sacrament. That means it is a *sign* and a *symbol*. It is a *sign* of the unity of Christ and the church. The dictionary tells us that a sign "suggests the presence or existence of a fact, condition or quality not immediately evident." A Christian marriage suggests the presence of a loving relationship between Christ and the body of Christ. Beyond that, marriage is a *symbol*. A symbol points to a reality and simultaneously participates in that reality. Marriage is a symbol in that it points to and becomes a part of Christ's relationship with the people of God, while Christ's relationship with the people of God becomes part of a marriage.

That rather complex theology might be stated more simply: in marriage, we encounter Christ in a way we do not encounter Christ anywhere else. Obviously, marriage is not the only place we encounter Christ, but in the marriage relationship we do so in a way that is different from how we encounter Christ in worship, in parental love, in nature, or in other parts of our lives. A key (although not only) aspect of what makes the marriage encounter different is that we have made a public, lifelong commitment of unconditional love, just as Christ's life, death, resurrection, and promise to be with us always (Matt. 28:20) is a public, eternity-long commitment of unconditional love. Our commitment in marriage is only a small sign of that great love. And yet our marriage becomes a powerful symbol to us and to the world because we bear witness to Christ's love, and Christ's presence in our lives becomes love in our midst.

Being married makes a difference. Not that God loves you any more or less. Being married makes a difference because it is an opportunity for you to experience Christ's love in that relationship and it is an opportunity for that relationship to "show forth" Christ's love to others.

> # QUESTIONS FOR COUPLES
> # TO DISCUSS

› Marriage Preparation

- How did you respond as you read each of the sections in this chapter?

- Are you ready to continue the journey into this marriage now? ever? Do you want to wait? Decide not to go on?

- If you do not want to proceed with the wedding, how will you tell your partner? How will you tell others? What will you need to do to cancel any existing plans? What support will you need and how will you get that support?

- How will you react if your partner does not want to proceed with the wedding? What support would you need and how would you get that support?

- If you are uncertain about whether to proceed or not, what do you think is creating the feelings of uncertainty? Who or what might help you resolve your ambivalence? If you decide to wait a while, what changes would you want to see? How would you go about working on the issues? What support will you need during this time and how will you get that support?

- If your partner is uncertain about whether to proceed or not, how would you react? What would you do? What support would you need and how would you get that support?

- If you are wondering "Why bother?" with getting married, how will you tell you partner? How do you think the two of you will deal with it? What if your partner asks, "Why bother?" How will you react? Who or what might help you in this situation?

- How satisfied are you with your relationship? What is your assessment of your relationship so far? Give it a numerical score between 1 (low) and 100 (high). Then write a paragraph describing it. What does doing this tell you about yourself and your partner?

- If your assessment of your relationship is lower than you want, what will you do about it? Decide how you will discuss this with your partner. What support will you need and how will you get that support? What if your partner's assessment is low: how will you react? What support would you need and how would you get that support?

- Make a list of at least ten things that you believe would improve your relationship. Decide how you will discuss these items with your partner.

- Make a list of at least twenty-five things you most value about your relationship— qualities, experiences, aspects of your relationship you want to celebrate. Choose a few items from your list that you would like to do more of, do again, or increase.

- Read the statement from the prayer book quoted at the beginning of this chapter. How do you feel you and your partner are "entering into" this marriage? What can you do or do you want to do to enter into it reverently?

- What did you learn from this chapter? What decisions do you choose to make in response to what you learned?

🕉 Marriage Enrichment

- How did you respond as you read each of the sections in this chapter?

- Read the statement from the prayer book quoted at the beginning of the chapter. How do you feel you and your spouse "entered into" your marriage? Has that changed over time? If so, how?

- How satisfied are you with your marriage? What is your assessment of your marriage so far? Give it a numerical score between 1 (low) and 100 (high). Then write a paragraph describing it. What does doing this tell you about yourself and your marriage?

- If your assessment of your marriage is lower than you want, what will you do about it? Decide how you will discuss this with your spouse. What support will you need and how will you get that support? What if your spouse's assessment is low: how will you react? What support would you need and how would you get that support?

- Make a list of at least ten things that you believe would improve your marriage. Decide how you will discuss these items with your spouse.

- Make a list of at least twenty-five things you most value about your marriage—qualities, experiences, aspects of your marriage you want to celebrate. Choose a few items from your list that you would like to do more of, do again, or increase.

- Are you committed to continuing the journey in this marriage? How committed would you rate yourself on a scale of 1 to 100?

- If you are considering divorce, whose counsel will you seek in the church? How have you tried to preserve your marriage? What would you like to try? What support will you need and how will you get that support?

- If you are uncertain or uneasy about your marriage, what do you think is creating those feelings? Who or what might help you resolve your ambivalence or identify the underlying issues? If your spouse is uncertain or uneasy, how would you react?

- If you are basically satisfied with your marriage and committed to continuing in it, what will you do to celebrate?

- What did you learn from this chapter? What decisions do you choose to make in response to what you learned?

QUESTIONS FOR GROUPS
TO DISCUSS

As you discuss the following questions, please be aware that one or more couples in the group may be struggling with the difficult decision of whether to proceed with their wedding, to work on serious issues within their relationship, or even to end their marriage. Be sensitive to how they will hear the discussion. Do not put pressure on anyone to discuss a decision that may be too painful to talk about right now. Do be open and available to listen if anyone decides to talk.

If one of the couples volunteers the information that they have decided not to proceed with the wedding, to seek marital counseling, or to divorce, or that they are trying to decide what to do, it is important that you be as supportive as possible. Do not give advice or try to make their decisions for them. Listen to them. Assure them that you care about them, will be there for them, and will pray for and love them in the days ahead.

- Discuss your responses to the readings under each of the four options: "Yes!" "No" "Maybe" "Why bother?" What would you say to a couple who found themselves in each section? What would you want someone to say to you or do for you if you found yourself making any of those choices?

- When do you think it might be good for a couple to wait before getting married? What might lead a couple to decide not to get married at all?

- What feelings do you think a couple would have if they decided not to get married or decided to wait? What do you think they could do to deal with those feelings? If you had decided not to get married, how would you have grieved the loss of that dream? How would you deal with family and friends?

- What if one partner wants to go ahead and the other does not? How might a couple work that out?

- What is your understanding of when divorce is appropriate? Do you think that assuming that divorce is an option tends to make it a self-fulfilling prophecy (which is the authors' opinion)? What can a couple do to prevent divorce?

- Read the Canon on the Dissolution of Marriage quoted in one of the boxes in this chapter. What counsel could the church give? If a couple you cared about was considering divorce, what could you offer them? If you think of yourself in that situation, what do you think would be helpful and what would make matters worse?

- What is your understanding of "making a lifelong commitment of unconditional love"? How can you commit to an unknown future? What is your understanding unconditional love?

- Read the statement from the prayer book quoted at the beginning of this chapter. What can you a couple do to enter into marriage reverently? How do you feel you and your partner "entered into" or will enter into your marriage?

- What did assessing your marriage/relationship and your satisfaction with it tell you about yourself and your relationship? Did you find the assessment useful? Did you make any decisions about changes you want to make as a couple or individually that you want to share with the group?

- If a couple's assessment of their marriage is lower than they want, what might they do about it? What support do you think they could get from the clergy in your church? from this group? from others in the congregation or the community?

- Share some of the items from your list of things you most value about your relationship—qualities, experiences, aspects of your marriage/relationship you want to celebrate. Are there any items on someone else's list that you want to add to yours?

- What are some ways a couple can celebrate their marriage? When and how often do you think celebration is in order? Why is celebrating your marriage important?

- In the wedding service we pray that "all married persons who have witnessed these vows may find their lives strengthened and their loyalties confirmed." Do you experience that when you attend weddings? Have you experienced that in this group?

- What did you learn from this chapter and discussion? What decisions did you make that you want to share with the group?

SUGGESTED PROJECTS

- Take a day and go off by yourself to some place that gives you privacy and peace. Spend time thinking and praying about your relationship or marriage. Take four sheets of paper and write on each one all the things that could lead you to say "yes," "no," "maybe," or "why bother?" Look at each list and project them ten years into the future. Is this who you are and who you want to be? As you imagine yourself ten years from now in this relationship, do you feel closer or more distant from your partner? from yourself? from God? If any of your answers to these questions are not what you want for yourself, decide what you will do. Write down your plan of action. Decide who or what you will need to support you and how you will get that support.

TEN

The Journey Ahead

Make their life together a sign of Christ's love to this sinful and broken world, that unity may overcome estrangement, forgiveness heal guilt, and joy conquer despair.
(BCP 429)

A marriage is a journey. The wedding service is only one stop on that journey. Your marriage journey began the moment the two of you met. It has and will continue to grow and build over time.

The image of the journey is important, especially in this world of instant gratification where people tend to expect quick results and complete satisfaction. Marriage is not like a television show, where the characters are introduced, the drama is built, and the problems are identified and then neatly solved—all within the thirty-minute time slot! Love and life are slower, happening on several levels at the same time. Often we can only see progress in hindsight.

Think about going on a long journey across a continent or around the world. Imagine what it would be like. Sometimes you travel across flatlands with wide open spaces where you can see where you are headed. At other times you find yourself in forests where your vision of where you have been and where you are going is obscured. At still other times you sail across deep lakes and ford fast-flowing streams, cross endless deserts and climb impossibly high mountains.

A marriage is like that. The terrain keeps changing and we are constantly offered new choices. Do we run when the ground is flat? Should we swim across the lake or go around it? Can we make it over that mountain? Do we have enough water to make it across the desert? You need to plan for love and life the way you plan for a trip. Look for maps that tell you where you are. Figure out how to read the signs. Develop and use traveling skills. Be open to learning new skills. Ask for help when you get lost or stuck.

You also have some choices about how you want to live the marriage journey. As when you travel, you can choose to take the quickest, easiest route to your destination. You can both learn map reading, driving, hiking, climbing, or water/food locating skills, divide the duties, or depend on one of you to do all of the work. You can spend your time fighting with each other and never notice where you've been, where you are, or where you're going. You can sit down in one spot and never see the rest of what is ahead. Or you can choose to enjoy the journey!

Enjoying the journey means different things to different people. For us, it means being aware of what each place along the way has to offer. The flatland can be boring or it can reveal a wide expanse of sky that is overwhelmingly beautiful. Climbing the mountain can be exhausting and frightening until we look up and see the view in the distance or look down and see the wonderful creatures at our feet, stop to appreciate them, and celebrate the triumph of what we accomplished thus far. The desert can seem dry and dull until we stop to look at the tiny insects that thrive in the desolation, the cactus that blooms,

> ### Building a Marriage
>
> *For which of you, intending to build a tower, does not first sit down and estimate the cost, to see whether he has enough to complete it? Otherwise, when he has laid the foundation and is not able to finish, all who see it will begin to ridicule him, saying, "This fellow began to build and was not able to finish."*
> (Luke 14:28-30)
>
> Building a marriage is costly: it takes time and effort and requires sacrifices and dedication. You don't start building a house or embark on a trip without making sure you have what you need to finish it—or at least an idea of where you are going to get it. So too, building a marriage requires "counting the cost" and making a commitment to doing what is required to get the resources needed to finish the job.

the gradations in the grains of sand. Suddenly the desert comes alive; its silence touches a space within us.

Our marriage journey has taken us some interesting places, just as yours has. The trick is to find ways to travel along the road in a way that allows each of you to enjoy the changing scenery and to draw what is most positive out of every part of the journey. We do that by not expecting the scenery to be what we want it to be, but by letting it be what it is and learning to discover and appreciate its inherent beauty.

We both like older people and often find ourselves smiling when we see the tender love an elderly couple expresses in their relationship. They know each other well, they've been through more together than we could ever guess, and they've respected and cared for their love over the years. We can see that because it shows in how they look at each other, touch each other, and help each other as they go up the stairs, across the room, and out the door. And as they leave, we look at each other and say, "We want to be like that when we're old." We want to be like that, rather than distant, tired, and empty—which we've also seen in older couples. Being like that at eighty or ninety means taking the time to care for your love daily.

In the marriage service we ask that God will "make their life together a sign of Christ's love." Christ loves us, and is able to see the beauty, the lovableness of each of us, each and every day. The marriage journey gives us the opportunity to travel through life together, as a sign of Christ's love to ourselves, to each other, and to the world.

We wish you Godspeed on your journey.

QUESTIONS FOR COUPLES
TO DISCUSS

❧ Marriage Preparation

- Discuss the journey metaphor. What does it tell you about yourself and your relationship? Talk about how each of you approaches actual trips. Does that tell you anything that might help you understand your marriage?

- What are your expectations regarding the first months of marriage life? the first year? What adjustments do you anticipate making?

- What are your expectations for how you will respond to the changes in scenery you are likely to encounter in the years ahead?

- What are your plans for taking time together daily? weekly? at set times during the year? What do you want to do during that time? How will you guard that personal time together as the pressures mount over the years?

- What is your picture of how you will be old together?

- How do you think your life together will be a sign of Christ's love?

- What are your expectations regarding the wedding—preparations, the service, showers, costs, families, the honeymoon? Identify potential problems and discuss ways to address them. Discuss specific service questions and work with the clergy and/or others designated to assist you in planning the service.

- What are the most significant things you have learned in reading and discussing this book? What are the most significant decisions you have made? Think about how you might want to remind yourself of what you have learned and decided. You might, for example, plan to look back on your first anniversary and on subsequent anniversaries to see how your perceptions have changed.

❧ Marriage Enrichment

- Discuss the journey metaphor. What does it tell you about yourself and your marriage? Talk about how each of you approaches actual trips. Does that tell you anything that might help you understand your marriage?

- When you got married, what were your expectations for how you would respond to the changes in scenery in the years after the wedding? What were your expectations regarding the first months of marriage life? the first couple of years? What adjustments did you anticipate making? How accurate were your expectations? What adjustments did you actually make? How did you respond to the changes?

- Do you take time together daily? weekly? at set times during the year? What do you do during that time? How have you guarded that personal time together as the pressures mounted over the years?

- What is your picture of how you will be old together?

- How do you think your life together has been and can be a sign of Christ's love?

- What are the most significant things you have learned in reading and discussing this book? What are the most significant decisions you have made? Think about how you might want to remind yourself of what you have learned and decided. You might, for example, plan to look back at this time a year from now or on your wedding anniversaries to review what you learned and decided and to see how your perceptions have changed.

QUESTIONS FOR GROUPS TO DISCUSS

- Discuss the journey metaphor. What does it tell you about yourself and your marriage? Talk about how you approach actual trips. Does that tell you anything that might help you understand your marriage? If this metaphor does not seem to work for some group members, identify and discuss other metaphors for marriage.

- What are your expectations for how you will respond to the changes in scenery you are likely to encounter in the years ahead? What can you or will you do to make the journey more interesting and enjoyable?

- What are your plans for taking time together daily? weekly? at set times during the year? What do you want to do during that time? How will you guard that personal time together as the pressures mount over the years?

- What is your picture of how you will be old together?

- How do you think your life together will be a sign of Christ's love?

- What are the most significant things you have learned in reading and discussing this book? What are the most significant decisions you have made?

- Spend some time talking about how your experience together as a group has been for each of you. Talk about how you might support each other after the group ends. Evaluate the book, the group, and your leaders by giving honest feedback on what has been helpful and what was not helpful. Thank those who have given you the gift of time, honesty, insight, and support. Say goodbye.

Resources

LIST OF BOOKS AND ORGANIZATIONS

We believe that the best resources you have available to you are other people: your clergyperson, lay people in your congregations, various professionals in your community, family, and friends. However, we also have some books to suggest. You can find innumerable good books in any of the following categories; these are just a few suggestions to get you started.

ॐ **Abuse or Addiction**

- Patricia Evans, *The Verbally Abusive Relationship* (Holbrook, Mass.: Bob Evans Publisher, 1992).

  Designed to help women identify if they are experiencing verbal abuse and to develop effective strategies to address this problem.

- Robert J. Ackerman and Susan E. Pickering, *Before It's Too Late* (Deerfield Beach, Fl.: Health Communications, 1995).

  Addresses problems of abuse and addiction; can help to identify if you are in such a relationship, what to do, and where to get help.

The following organizations can provide information or help you find a local group; *they are not hotlines.* If you are in immediate distress, call 911, the police, a local women's shelter, child protective agency, or other state or social service agency. Local self-help groups such as AA and Al-Anon are generally listed in your local phone book.

- Child Help
  6463 Independence Avenue
  Woodland Hills, CA 91367
  800-422-4453
  (information and referrals regarding child abuse)

- National Resource Center on Domestic Violence
  6400 Frank Drive, Suite 1300
  Harrisburg, PA 17112-2778
  800-537-2238
  (information regarding spouse/partner abuse)

- Center for the Prevention of Sexual and Domestic Violence
  1914 North 34th, Suite 105
  Seattle, WA 98103-9058
  206-634-1903
  (An interreligious educational ministry that serves as a resource to congregations that wish to address the religious issues relevant to sexual and domestic violence.)

- Family Services of America Information and Referral
  800-221-2681
  (information on abuse, addiction, relationship difficulties; referrals to local counseling agencies)

- Alcoholics Anonymous
  World Services, Inc.
  475 Riverside Drive
  New York, NY 10115
  212-870-3400
  (information and referrals to local AA groups)

- Al-Anon Family Group Headquarters
  P. O. Box 182 / Madison Square Station
  New York, NY 10159
  800-344-2666 or 212-302-7240
  (information and referrals to local Al-Anon groups for families and friends of alcoholics)

- Narcotics Anonymous
  P. O. Box 9999
  Van Nuys, CA 91409
  818-773-9999
  (information and referrals to local NA groups)

- Nar-Anon Family Groups
  P. O. Box 2562
  Palos Verdes, CA 90274-0119
  310-547-5800
  (information and referrals to local Nar-Anon groups)

ဢ Children

- Elizabeth M. Whelan, *A Baby...Maybe?* (New York: Bobbs-Merrill Company, 1975).
  A guide to deciding whether to have children. A bit dated, but covers all the issues.

- Melinda Blau, *Families Apart: Ten Keys to Successful Co-Parenting* (New York: The Berkeley Publishing Group, 1993).
  Solid guidance on how to maintain a productive parenting relationship with your ex-spouse.

- Karne Savage and Patricia Adams, *The Good Stepmother* (New York: Avon Books, 1988).
  A clear picture of what to expect and how best to respond to the joys and difficulties of step-parenting.

ဢ Communication

- John Gray, *Men Are From Mars, Women Are From Venus* (New York: HarperCollins, 1994).
  A description of differences in communication styles of men and women. Not well written and a bit overdone in our opinion, but worth it for the metaphor alone!

- Deborah Tannen, *You Just Don't Understand* (New York: Ballantine Books, 1990).
  Differences in male and female communication styles; well-written and helpful.

- Riki Robbins Jones, *Negotiating Love* (New York: Ballantine Books, 1995).
  Communication difficulties and ways to negotiate a mutually beneficial reso-lution to problems.

⁞ Family Patterns
- John Bradshaw, *Bradshaw On the Family* (Deerfield Beach, Fl.: Health Communications, 1988).
  Describes functional and dysfunctional family systems and strategies for addressing problems resulting from learned behavior patterns. Unfortunately, Bradshaw tends to see everyone's family as emotionally impaired. He does, however, help to identify problematic patterns.

- Edwin H. Friedman, *Generation to Generation* (New York: Guilford Press, 1985).
  The first couple of chapters give an overview of family systems and how behavior patterns are passed from one generation to the next. This book is pretty heavy reading, especially beyond the opening section.

⁞ Life Changes
- William Bridges, *Transitions* (Reading, Mass.: Addison-Wesley Publishing Company, 1980).
  Describes the dynamics of transition times and identifies strategies for coping with changes in life.

- Edward Gleason, Dying We Live (Cambridge, Mass.: Cowley Publications, 1990).
  Explores the many dimensions of transition and loss through the words of the Book of Common Prayer's burial office.

⁞ Marital Instruments
- David Olson, Joan Druckman, and David Fournier, *Prepare/Enrich* (Minneapolis, Minn.: Life Innovations, Inc.).
  An inventory of 125 items assessing strength and growth areas with a seminar; used with premarital and marital workshops. Training (which can be expensive) is required for use. Contact Life Innovations, Inc. / P.O. Box 190 / Minneapolis, MN 55440-0190 / (612) 331-1731.

- Susan Adams, *The Marital Compatibility Test* (Secaucus, N.J.: Carol Publishing Group, 1995).

  Seventeen sometimes humorous multiple choice questionnaires about many of the issues, large and small, mentioned in our book. Especially good for anyone not living together.

- David Kiersey and Marilyn Bates, *Please Understand Me* (Del Mar, Calif.: Prometheus Nemesis Book Company, 1978, 1984).

  Many people use the Myers Briggs Type Indicator (MBTI) to help couples understand personality differences (requires a certified administrator). This book includes the Kiersey Temperament Sorter, which is based on the MBTI and can be done by anyone; also has a good chapter on marital compatibility.

℔ Marriages

- Edward Gleason, Redeeming Marriage (Cambridge, Mass.: Cowley Publications, 1988).

  A fine meditation on the marriage service in the Book of Common Prayer.

- Harville Hendrix and Helen Hunt, *The Couples Companion: Meditations and Exercises for Getting the Love You Want* (New York: Pocket Books, 1994).

  One page for every day of the year giving a quotation, brief reflection, a project, and a meditation suggestion to help couples deepen their relationship.

- Maggie Scarf, *Intimate Partners: Patterns in Love and Marriage* (New York: Random House, 1987).

  Delves into the causes of marital difficulties and suggests ways to address them. Useful to both married couples and those engaged in marital counseling.

- Susan Page, *Now that I'm Married, Why Isn't Everything Perfect?* (New York: Dell Books, 1994).

  Describes "the eight essential traits of couples who thrive" and gives suggestions on how to develop those traits and build solid marriage.

- John Gottman, *Why Marriages Succeed or Fail...And How You Can Make Yours Last* (New York: Simon & Schuster, 1994).

  Designed to help you identify your marriage type, assess the strengths and weaknesses in your marriage, and suggest specific actions you can take to build your marital relationship.

ಸಿ Money

- Susan Forward and Craig Buck, *Money Demons* (New York: Bantam Books, 1994).

  Describes emotionally driven money difficulties (debt, depravation, gambling, reckless spending, unbalanced incomes) and strategies for coping with them.

The authors appreciate the assistance of several clergy and lay people engaged in premarital and marital counseling who use and recommended many of the resources outlined here. Most were participants in an online meeting on marriage preparation on the Quest computer network serving the Anglican Communion.

ORGANIZING AND LEADING GROUPS

The following suggestions are intended to assist clergy and congregations in establishing marriage preparation groups, marriage enrichment groups, or married couple retreats. We have also included a few general suggestions for those leading study groups. A more detailed training program for marriage mentors and a retreat design are available from LeaderResources (see the last page of this chapter). These congregational, regional, or diocesan groups may be led by clergy, lay people, or teams of both.

🙲 Marriage Mentors

We are using the term "marriage mentors" for married couples who agree to work with those about to be married or with those seeking enrichment of their marriage. The role of marriage mentors includes leading a marriage preparation or marriage enrichment group or retreat and/or providing individual mentoring. It does not include leading adult education groups.

Marriage mentors should be carefully selected and trained before they begin their work. The best marriage mentors are couples with a healthy marriage and a strong faith life. They should be regular participants in the life of the church and generally recognized in the community as having a good marriage. They must be good listeners and good at restraining themselves from giving advice. They must be willing to share some of their own story without making their story the centerpiece or the norm for how others should act.

The role of marriage mentors is to lead the discussion (set the context, ask questions, encourage people to talk), to listen, to love, and to pray for those with whom they work. It is important that marriage mentors understand that they are not counselors and they are not responsible for fixing others couples' problems. They should never give advice beyond encouraging people to seek help. They must be discreet and never discuss private information outside the meeting or their supervisory sessions with the clergy. They should regularly report to the clergy on the group's progress, on their assessment of each couples' readiness for marriage, and especially on any serious problems they feel need to be addressed by the clergy.

❧ Suggestions for Leading Meetings

We have given group discussion questions for each chapter, but encourage group leaders to plan their gatherings carefully and not just ask those questions. Read the chapter beforehand and identify with which questions you want to start and with which ones you want to end. Put a star next to any question you feel is a "must discuss question" so you can make sure to ask it before the time is over. Think about and make a note of any additional questions you might want to raise.

When you begin the first meeting, outline what you will do, how long the meetings will be, and what norms will govern the group's behavior. Always suggest that the group agree that whatever is said in the group will be kept confidential except for your reports to your supervising clergyperson. Other norms to suggest are: starting and ending on time, being open and honest, speaking only for oneself ("I think" rather than "my partner says" or "they say"), not pressuring people to talk about anything they don't want to discuss, respecting each other, acknowledging that everyone has a right to their feelings and opinions. You will need to settle the question of smoking and refreshments. Invite the group to add any other issues they might agree upon and check to make sure everyone agrees to the list (it is best if this list is written and posted in some visible spot).

Begin each group meeting with a time of worship, perhaps using the Daily Devotions on page 137ff. in the *Book of Common Prayer*. You might also want to use one of the scripture passages from that session's chapter. You then may want to give a brief (three to five minute) summary of the chapter's content or simply read some or all of the chapter.[1] This is especially important if you have a group where several people are consistently unprepared. If possible, give one brief relevant story or example from your own life as part of the summary or as a supplement to the reading. Select stories that are relevant but not inappropriately revealing. You want to encourage people to share personal information, but it is important to remember that "letting it all hang out" can be damaging. Don't say anything that would embarrass

---

1   If you plan to read the chapter, make sure you check with the group. Many people are rightly annoyed by having to listen to something they have already read. On the other hand, you may want to remind them that hearing something read aloud often allows us to hear different things. That difference and the refresher benefit may make reading the chapter or excerpts from it useful. Just make sure the group agrees to this strategy after the first meeting.

you or your spouse if someone later talked about it elsewhere (despite the confidentiality rule, you can never be sure).

Your opening question might be to invite people to react to the chapter and their discussion of the questions for couples. Then use questions from the book or your own list, according to what seems appropriate at the time. Encourage people to listen to each other, to identify options, and to explore the pros and cons of various options rather than to tell each other what to think or do. Insist that each person must make his or her own decisions. Do not let the group or yourself fall into giving advice, even when someone asks. If someone says "What do you think I should do?" respond: "Only you can decide what you should do. However, we can help you identify some of the different options you can choose from."

The book uses passages from the marriage service, so it would be helpful to have copies of the *Book of Common Prayer* available to look them up. Over the weeks, the couples will become increasingly familiar with the service, which will help those planning their wedding and serve as a reminder for those already married. Some participants who are not Episcopalians may be unfamiliar with this book and will need page numbers and explanations. If you have couples from different denominations you may want to get copies of their books of worship to compare and contrast services.

In addition to providing information and keeping the conversation moving, your job is to set boundaries. Do not allow anyone to make fun of, ridicule, or tease someone else in the group. Do not allow people to become judgmental or assume that they, and they alone, have all the answers. Do not let someone take on the counselor or "preacher" role. Encourage people to listen to and respect each other. If an individual or a couple seems to be having difficulty (upset, crying, angry) you may want to speak with them outside the group meeting and perhaps suggest they meet with the clergy as well.

It may take a while before people begin to talk on a significant level. Be patient. Trust takes time. If you create an environment in which it is safe to talk, people generally will do so. Then you may find the opposite difficulty—getting them to stop! If someone is talking too much, you can gently interrupt and suggest that someone who hasn't spoken yet might respond to the question. If someone is revealing too much, you can again interrupt and suggest that it is not necessary to tell all of the details, but perhaps just give an overview. Adjust your next few questions to be less personal. For example, instead of asking "what did you..." ask "what do you think a couple might do...." This creates more emotional distance that can help someone revealing too much regain his or her personal boundaries.

If not having enough time for discussion and sharing is an issue, you may want to ask the group if they want to extend their meeting time another fifteen minutes. Usually ninety minutes is about the right time for a group session. It is often better to keep them wanting more than to go too long and thus deplete their energy before the last session.

Close your meeting with a time of prayer; again, the Daily Devotions or, if it is evening, Compline (BCP 127) would be appropriate. It is often helpful to pray for each person by name. Either you can do that as leader or you may want to join hands and offer prayers around the circle with each person praying for the person on his or her right. If at all possible we encourage you to make this closing time a time when everyone has a chance to pray so couples who might not be used to praying together may become more comfortable doing that. If you open with an invitation for general prayers (anyone prays in any order) and then close with the individual prayers (around the circle for each person), you can include those who are comfortable with praying and yet provide a way for those who are less comfortable to participate. If you choose to do this, explain it carefully the first time and suggest what they might say (for example, "Lord, bless XX as she prepares for marriage"). Remember, some people may never have prayed aloud before, so make it easier for them to start by suggesting something that is very brief.

Finally, we encourage you to remember the couples you mentor in your daily prayers. Pray for each person by name. If you have identified specific problems, ask for God's assistance for them; if you see strengths, give thanks for them. Perhaps the two most important things you can do for the couple you mentor are pray for them and work on your own marriage. These couples will see you as models of what it means to be a Christian couple living in a Christian marriage, so do not neglect your marriage or your faith life. Being a marriage mentor is a ministry. Seek God's help in your work and give thanks for this gift of ministry offered to you.

∾ Marriage Preparation or Enrichment Retreats

Most of what was said above will apply to leading a retreat program. The primary adjustments you will need to make concern timing and the amount of material covered during the retreat versus read beforehand. Also, if you have a large group, you will need to assemble a team to lead the retreat. One or two couples can provide the primary leadership, with other couples leading smaller discussion groups of about five couples. Other team members might lead the worship, music, and any fun elements you want to add. Still others might handle logistics (meals, snacks, rooms, registration, furniture arrangements, trouble shooting).

If couples attending the retreat are honestly committed to reading the book and doing the couples' questions ahead of time, you can schedule more group discussion time for each chapter. However, realistically, most groups will not have done that and will want to use this time to read, digest, and work on the material.

If this is the case, we recommend you combine several chapters. If you are starting on Friday night, you can cover the introduction and chapter on *The Sacrament of Marriage*. On Saturday morning you may want to combine *Extended Families* and *Being with Others* for the opening session and then combine *Living Together* and *Fighting Fair* for the session just before a late lunch or right after an early lunch. *Money Matters* and *The Gift of Children* probably need their own sessions on Saturday afternoon, with *Sexual Intimacy* by itself on Saturday evening. Sunday morning can begin with a combined session on *Yes, No, Maybe, Why Bother?* and *The Journey Ahead*, leading logically to a closing Eucharist just before a late lunch or after an early lunch. If you have more time on Sunday you can add more break time into the schedule. Each session would probably begin with a brief talk, a summary of the chapter(s) and/or a reading of excerpts, followed by time for couples to complete and discuss the couples' questions. That section would then close with a group session (or several groups of about five couples each).[2]

A retreat is a time of intensity that often magnifies emotions. While this is good, it also holds the potential for problems. It is important that your information about a marriage enrichment retreat makes clear that it is not a "fix it" event for those with troubled marriages, but an enrichment event for those with basically healthy marriages. It is also helpful to have experienced and trained group leaders. In addition, it would be wise to include a clergyperson serving as a chaplain and/or a trained counselor on the leadership team. Above all, make sure the leaders do not attempt to counsel couples, give advice, or present themselves as trained in marital counseling (unless this is actually true). Retreat leaders are present to guide the group through a reflection process, to ask questions, to listen, to love, and to pray for participants.

℘ Education Groups

Education groups usually have different expectations and norms than the other groups we have described. They often meet on Sunday mornings for only forty-five minutes to an hour; that shorter timeframe changes the group dynamics and affects what can be covered in the time available. Education groups usually are "open," which

---

2 A detailed outline and suggestions for how to prepare and lead a retreat is available from LeaderResources. See the information provided at the end of this chapter.

means new members may join at any time. Many people attend education groups to learn something about a topic and are not prepared to be self-revelatory.

If you are leading an education group, remind yourself of how the group normally functions (if you are not the ongoing group leader, ask a previous group leader). Be aware of the previous level of intimacy and match it or clearly negotiate with the group before you ask the more personal questions. Do the same negotiations with a new group and in your information about the group before it meets. Unless the group wants to be more intimate and self-revelatory, select or adapt the questions to be less personal. Discuss the ideas and talk about what they have observed or what they believe a couple might do in various situations, rather than asking them to talk about their own relationships. (However, do not allow them to name or in some other way to identify other people or discuss others' problems in detail.) If you and the group decide to use the personal questions, read the suggestions for group leaders given above.

PRAYERS FOR COUPLES

ও A Prayer of Petition

Eternal God, creator and preserver of all life, author of salvation, and giver of all grace: Look with favor upon the world you have made, and for which your Son gave his life, and especially upon us whom you have made one flesh in Holy Matrimony.

Give us wisdom and devotion in the ordering of our common life, that we may be a strength to each other in need, a counselor in perplexity, a comfort in sorrow, and a companion in joy.

Grant that our wills may be so knit together in your will, and our spirits in your Spirit, that we may grow in love and peace with you and one another all the days of our life.

Give us grace, when we hurt each other, to recognize and acknowledge our fault, and to seek each other's forgiveness and yours.

Make our life together a sign of Christ's love to this sinful and broken world, that unity may overcome estrangement, forgiveness heal guilt, and joy conquer despair.

Bestow on us, if it is your will, the gift and heritage of children, and the grace to bring them up to know you, to love you, and to serve you.

Give us such fulfillment of our mutual affection that we may reach out in love and concern for others.

Grant that the bonds of our common humanity, by which all your children are united one to another, and the living to the dead, may be so transformed by your grace that your will may be done on earth as it is in heaven; where, O Father, with your Son and the Holy Spirit, you live and reign in perfect unity, now and for ever. Amen.

⁎ A Prayer of Thanksgiving

Most gracious God, we give you thanks for your tender love in sending Jesus Christ to come among us, to be born of a human mother, and to make the way of the cross to be the way of life. We thank you, also, for consecrating the union of man and woman in his Name.

By the power of your Holy Spirit, pour out the abundance of your blessing upon us. Defend us from every enemy. Lead us into all peace. Let our love for each other be a seal upon our hearts, a mantle about our shoulders, and a crown upon our foreheads.

Bless us in our work and in our companionship; in our sleeping and in our waking; in our joys and in our sorrows; in our life and in our death.

Finally, in your mercy, bring us to that table where your saints feast for ever in your heavenly home; through Jesus Christ our Lord, who with you and the Holy Spirit lives and reigns, one God, for ever and ever. Amen.

⁎ Prayers for Blessing

God the Father, God the Son, God the Holy Spirit, bless, preserve, and keep us; the Lord mercifully with his favor look upon us, and fill us with all spiritual benediction and grace; that we may faithfully live together in this life, and in the age to come have life everlasting. Amen.

O God, you have so consecrated the covenant of marriage that in it is represented the spiritual unity between Christ and his church: Send therefore your blessing upon us your servants, that we may so love, honor, and cherish each other in faithfulness and patience, in wisdom and true godliness, that our home may be a haven of blessing and peace; through Jesus Christ our Lord, who lives and reigns with you and the Holy Spirit, one God, now and for ever. Amen.

God the Father, God the Son, God the Holy Spirit, bless, preserve, and keep us; the Lord mercifully with his favor look upon us, and fill us with all spiritual benediction and grace; that we may faithfully live together in this life, and in the age to come have life everlasting. Amen.

TRAINING PROGRAMS AND MATERIALS FOR GROUPS

Training programs and materials for those leading groups of couples are available from *LeaderResources*, including step-by-step instructions for the sessions and providing suggestions on how you might establish marriage preparation and marriage enrichment programs in your congregation. This resource is available in two forms: photocopiable masters and computer disk versions with templates you can adapt and customize with your church name and the couples' names. You receive the master copy and/or disk and a license allowing you to make as many copies as are needed.

 & **Leader's guide and participant materials for leadership training for:**
  - Marriage mentors to work with premarital couples, groups, or retreats.
  - Leadership teams to lead marriage enrichment groups or retreats.
  - Education group leaders for adult education programs.

& **The materials packet includes:**
  - All the questions in the book with write-in spaces that you can use as handouts.
  - Budgeting forms for the chapter on money.
  - Service booklets and bulletins for the marriage ceremony in the *Book of Common Prayer*, with or without Eucharist, an order of marriage, and the blessing of a civil marriage (computer templates can be modified or customized).
  - Ways to include children or step-children in weddings (computer templates are ready to "cut and paste" into bulletins or service booklets).
  - Brochures (photocopy master copy or adapt template to fit your situation):
    Selecting Scripture for your wedding.
    Selecting music for your wedding.
    Celebrating the Eucharist at your wedding.
    What is a blessing of a civil marriage?
    For parents and close family members.
    For attendants.
    For photographers.
  - Promotional materials for marital enrichment groups or retreats that you can use or modify (bulletin inserts, newsletter articles, invitations, poster, etc.).

For further information contact
LeaderResources
1-800-941-2218